A STATUE FOR MARY: THE SEACOLE LEGACY

BY LORD SOLEY AND OTHERS

EDITOR: JEAN GRAY

A STATUE FOR MARY:
THE SEACOLE LEGACY

UN Photo/JC McIlwaine

FOREWORD

When I was asked to chair the panel to choose an artist who would create a statue of Mary Seacole in London, I was delighted. Why? Because she was an unsung heroine, a Jamaican businesswoman, traveller and healer who wanted to go to Crimea to help treat the wounded and save lives. But she was refused by the authorities. Rather than accept defeat she went, independently, using her own money. Mary Seacole's experiences and the fact that she had been forgotten became the subject of discussion in Britain's black community. So a campaign to recognise her was born.

But what would be a fitting tribute to Mary Seacole? Artists were asked to submit their ideas and the panel interviewed a shortlist. It wasn't easy. We wanted to be true to her and her history. We wanted something fitting and memorable. The artists had very different ideas of how they saw her, as did the panel. Through a process of dialogue and sometimes disagreement we reached a decision. It was a fascinating process that resulted in the choice of Martin Jennings. His design encapsulated Mary Seacole's courage, compassion and connectivity between different but related cultures.

Clive Soley chaired the Mary Seacole Memorial Statute Appeal which raised the money. Clive and the Appeal's Trustees have done a fantastic job, never giving up in spite of the difficulties they faced over 12 years. The Trustees were inspired and supported by hundreds of community activists and a team of Ambassadors who contributed to that campaign. It has been a long haul but the commitment and dedication of all those involved has paid off.

There is a statue to Mary Seacole in the grounds of St Thomas' Hospital, a tribute to her life and work and her status as an important role model today. Thanks are due to the management and staff at Guy's and St Thomas' NHS Foundation Trust for agreeing to host the statue in such a beautiful setting. The organisations and individuals whose donations and hard work have kept the vision alive can now take ownership of the statue and continue Mary's legacy into the future.

Valerie Amos
The Right Honourable Baroness Amos CH PC

INTRODUCTION

A statue celebrating the life of Mary Seacole, the nurse of Jamaican and Scottish descent, best known for her brave and compassionate work with soldiers and sailors during the 19th Century Crimean War, was unveiled in London on June 30th 2016.

Sculptor Martin Jennings' stunning work is the first statue of a named black woman in the UK. It sits in the grounds of St Thomas' Hospital, opposite the Houses of Parliament on London's Southbank, among the beautiful artworks that give so much pleasure to St Thomas' patients, visitors and staff.

The statue was made possible by the donations and fundraising efforts of thousands of individual supporters as well as organisations large and small. This commemorative book describes the 12-year campaign to make it happen, in the words of those who have been most closely involved. It outlines the sculptor's vision for London's latest landmark and reveals how Mary's work will live on through the new Mary Seacole Trust.

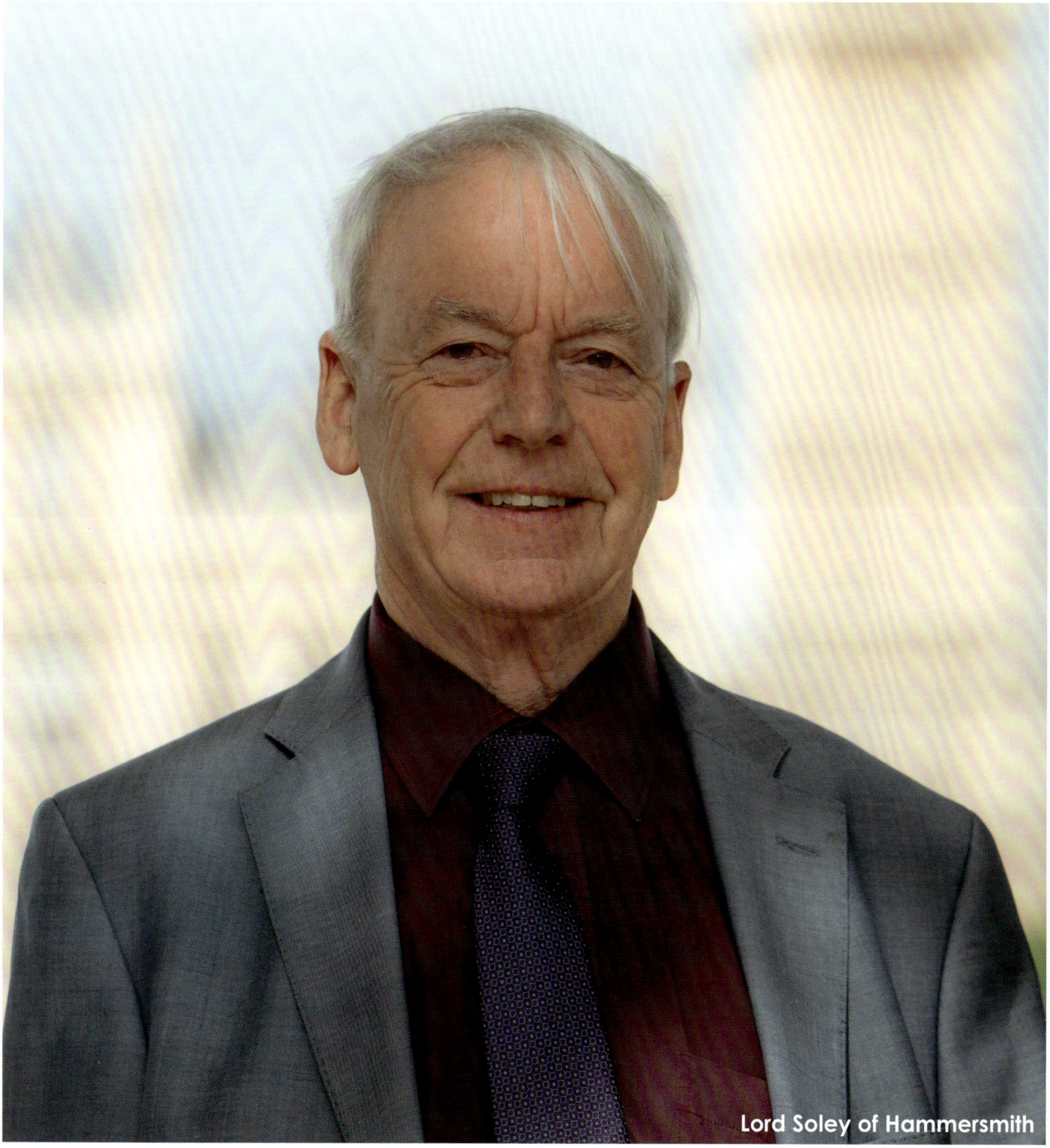
Lord Soley of Hammersmith

MARY SEACOLE MEMORIAL STATUE APPEAL

FROM A NORTH WEST LONDON CEMETERY TO THE SOUTHBANK

By Lord Soley of Hammersmith

Shortly after I was elected as the MP for Hammersmith in 1979 I was approached by the late Connie Mark MBE, BEM who together with a number of other women of Caribbean heritage had come to Britain at the beginning of World War II to help, as one of them put it, "the mother country in the fight for freedom". It was a remarkable statement and one that still fascinates me because the Caribbean islands were British colonies at the time. Jamaica did not become an independent state until 1962. As members of the Auxiliary Territorial Service they had helped maintain and clean the anti-aircraft guns on Wormwood Scrubs during the Second World War. They were proud of their war service.

They asked if I would join them at the grave of Mary Seacole in St Mary's Cemetery in Kensal Green where they held an annual memorial event. I listened to them talking about Mary Seacole and how she had not been included in the Crimean War memorials. They knew how popular she had been with the troops and with the wider British public and yet she had been airbrushed out of history. They wanted a statue to recognise her contribution and commitment to Britain and the British armed forces. You can read Mary Seacole's remarkable memoirs to see how important this was to her.

I made no comment at the time but resolved to try and organise a campaign in future years. When I decided to leave the House of Commons I set up the Mary Seacole Memorial Statue Appeal, thinking, naively, that it would cost some £50,000 and take a year or two to organise. How wrong I was! It has taken 12 years. The cost is well over £500,000 to cover not just the sculpture itself but also the additional costs of bringing a large public monument to completion. An enormous amount of work has been demanded of the Trustees and many other committed supporters. Contributions have come from schools, hospitals, and the general public. A number of companies, trade unions and other organisations, too many to mention but all are listed here in this book, have contributed very generously of time and money.

Mary Seacole had spent three days at the War Office trying to get permission to go to the Crimea to carry on the work she had done at the army's hospital in Jamaica. Did she give up when refused? No, she organised and paid for her own transport and set up the British Hotel in the Crimea where she covered her costs as a sutler, a person selling provisions to soldiers. She also used the knowledge inherited from her mother in the use of herbal remedies and nursing skills. Mary became a heroine of the troops and of Victorian society. She was praised in *The Times* newspaper and in the magazine *Punch*. When she returned bankrupt from the Crimea, the Army, led by a committee of senior officers and members of the Royal Family, organised concerts to raise funds and end her bankruptcy. Neither has today's Army forgotten her. I have letters of support with financial contributions to the statue from Army units whose forebears served in the Crimea. And now the Army nursing service has thrown its weight behind the campaign and will continue its involvement in the legacy programme.

Some people ask me 'Why a statue'? I might have asked the same question some years ago but I have learnt two important lessons from this. Firstly, the arts are not just important in their own right but the whole process of the campaign and the legacy are a real educational experience for all involved and for future generations. Secondly, Britain was not alone in 1939 and 1940. We had the support of those remarkable women who left their home in the Caribbean to come to Britain and help in our hour of need. These women were part of that vast reservoir of support for the ideas of freedom and democracy, no matter how complex in the context of Empire. Part of my motivation has been to get greater recognition of that contribution made by people from all parts of what was then the Empire and is now the Commonwealth.

There is a third reason for this statue. Statues of men are common, statues of women are less common but to my knowledge there is no statue of a named black women anywhere in the UK. We have now put that right. Britain is a remarkably tolerant multi racial society and no small part of that comes from our world history. You can see it now in our National Health Service which is why I am so pleased that Guy's and St Thomas' NHS Foundation Trust is hosting the statue on their ground opposite the Houses of Parliament. The future legacy programme will link up with the Florence Nightingale Museum, that other heroine of the Crimean War, and create a real learning experience for visitors who will be attracted by Martin Jennings' stunning depiction of Mary.

This long journey to recognise Mary Seacole has surmounted many problems but none so challenging as getting Martin Jennings and his small team to the Crimea to take an image of the ground where the British Hotel stood. This image was used to create the disc that stands behind the statue of Mary. The site of the British Hotel was not too far from the largest Russian Naval base in the world – and all this happened just months before the Russian occupation! The Ukrainian Ambassador in London was very co-operative as was the British Ambassador in Kiev. During the visit, Martin found pieces of porter bottles– British troops would cut the bottles open with a swipe of a sabre. There is real history encased in the large disc behind the statue that represents the world which Mary Seacole travelled so intrepidly. Mary Seacole triumphed over adversity. She did not let prejudice or disadvantage stand in her way. It is my hope that this impressive statue and the legacy programme will open the eyes of visitors from this country and the wider world to a remarkable woman at a remarkable time.

We should all recognise the international nature of our history, a history that has made the UK such a modern, diverse and dynamic society. Something to be proud of I think. Something that should be reflected in our art.

Clive Soley
Lord Soley of Hammersmith

Professor Elizabeth Anionwu CBE FRCN

MARY SEACOLE - HER LIFE

By Professor Elizabeth Anionwu CBE FRCN

'I trust that England will not forget one who nursed her sick, who sought out her wounded to aid and succour them, and who performed the last offices for some of her illustrious dead.'

This comment, written by *The Times* war correspondent Sir William Howard Russell in 1857, has been the motto of the Mary Seacole Memorial Statue Appeal.

Sir William mentioned Mary often, describing her work with soldiers on the battlefield, her bravery and kindness. But the quote above explains specifically why the Appeal's Trustees and supporters have refused to give up campaigning for the statue, in spite of the great difficulties encountered in raising sufficient funds.

Well known to her Victorian contemporaries, Mary somehow faded from history until the 1970s when Miss J Elise Gordon, Editor of the *Nursing Mirror*, located her burial place in Kensal Rise, North West London. As a result, the derelict grave was restored and reconsecrated, bringing together key organisations, including the British Commonwealth Nurses' War Memorial Fund, the Lignum Vitae Club (a London based group of Jamaican women), and the UK Jamaican Nurses' Association.

England may have forgotten Mary, but her rediscovery could not have been more timely. Her life, her views and her legacy have real meaning in modern, diverse Britain. That is why the statue, a lasting memorial and a major London landmark, stands as an inspiration to today's young people. Mary's story will remind future generations of what one woman achieved in spite of the obstacles she faced and the discrimination that she had to overcome in order to fulfil her mission of caring for soldiers on and off the battlefield. Much of what we know about Mary's life comes from her autobiography *Wonderful Adventures of Mrs Seacole in Many Lands*, written in 1857 with a new edition commissioned in 1984.

The daughter of a Creole mother and Scottish father, Mary Jane Grant was born in Kingston, Jamaica early in the 1800s - assumed to be around 1805 although she was always rather coy when discussing her exact date of birth. Little is known about her father except that he was a soldier from an 'old Scotch family'. Her mother kept a boarding house in Kingston and was described by Mary as 'an admirable doctress'. This joint inheritance of Scottish military 'pomp, pride and circumstance' alongside the knowledge she gained from assisting her mother in the care of invalid officers and their wives may help explain why Mary's destiny was to become one of history's best known military nurses.

In 1836, following two trips to England, Mary married Edwin Horatio Hamilton Seacole. Sadly, her husband became unwell and Mary was widowed after only eight years of marriage. With the loss of her mother shortly after, Mary was left to 'battle with the world as best I could'. And battle she did, travelling to Panama for the purpose of visiting her brother and setting up a boarding house. However, an outbreak of cholera in the gold-prospecting town of Cruces led to Mary employing her nursing skills single-handedly. Back in Jamaica and caring for victims of yellow fever, Mary was asked to supervise nursing services at Up-Park Camp, the British military headquarters in Kingston, an experience that would later influence her decision to head for the Crimean War.

A subsequent visit to London in the autumn of 1854 caused Mary to change course dramatically. She had been planning an ordinary business trip until she learned of the appalling care being offered to wounded soldiers in the Crimea and the campaign to recruit nurses to work under Florence Nightingale at Scutari Barrack Hospital in Turkey. Having missed Nightingale by just a few days, Mary determined not to give up and was seen in London by a colleague of Nightingale's who rejected her. Mary was deeply hurt by the blow, and it left her wondering whether racism was at the root of her rejection. But Mary was having none of it and she soon rallied.

At the age of 49, concern for her beloved soldiers drove her to employ her considerable entrepreneurial and networking skills so that by the spring of 1855 she had secured the funds necessary to take her to the Crimea under her own steam. Teaming up with a relative of her late husband's, Mr Thomas Day, Mary set up the 'British Hotel', a canteen and store very close to the war zone, where she also ran a morning dispensary before visiting sick and wounded soldiers in their huts or on the battlefield. When the war ended abruptly in 1856, Mary returned to London and was declared bankrupt. Key figures in the military and the media, together with members of the Royal Family, ensured she was not destitute. One example of their support and gratitude was the four-day

'Seacole Fund Grand Military Gala' held in July 1857 and attended by a total of 80,000 people. The venue was the magnificent Royal Surrey Gardens located in the centre of London on the banks of the River Thames. Mary died on 14 May 1881 at her home in Paddington. Her grave is in St Mary's Catholic Cemetery in Kensal Green, London. A short obituary appeared in *The Times*.

This statue, brought about by thousands of small acts of generosity, by the support of individuals from all walks of life, including many in the public eye, by trade unions and other organisations, is just one of the ways in which Mary has now regained her place in British history. In the school curriculum it is recommended that pupils learn about Mary Seacole. She is included alongside Florence Nightingale and she was named the Greatest Black Briton in a 2004 poll. Annual nursing awards – a joint venture between the Department of Health, professional organisations and trade unions – bear her name, as do numerous streets and buildings throughout the country. Her portrait has hung in the National Portrait Gallery since the 2005 bicentenary celebrations.

Mary Jane Grant Seacole's story is compelling and relevant. This is the first statue to a named black woman in the UK. That honour is bestowed upon the woman who took pride in her Jamaican and Scottish heritage, who condemned slavery and refused to accept discrimination. She overcame any obstacle that might stop her from delivering compassionate and skillful nursing care.

Professor Elizabeth Anionwu CBE FRCN, Emeritus Professor of Nursing, University of West London and Vice-Chair MSMSA

Martin Jennings FRBS

AGAINST A BATTLEFIELD

By Martin Jennings FRBS

Some years ago when I was first approached to develop an idea for a monument to the remarkable Mary Seacole, I wondered how I could represent meaningfully someone so different from me, who lived in a time so different from our own. I had read as much as I could about her, including the powerful autobiography detailing her nursing of British troops during the Crimean War. My imagination was filled with the image of an indomitable figure who repeatedly challenged and overcame the many obstacles placed in her path. But there was more to it than this. There were important symbolic strands in her story, apt for our own age, and they needed drawing together. This would be Britain's first statue of a named black woman. The moment would be highly charged.

A public sculpture needs to be appropriate to our own time if it is to be welcomed into our cultural landscape. It seemed to me that if I was to show Seacole's enduring relevance I would have to make a new kind of monument. I didn't want to sculpt a mere pastiche of Victorian statuary as it would leave her story seeming significant only to the history of the mid-nineteenth century. If however I could find some way of grounding her against a backdrop of her own time and place, as literally as possible, then paradoxically I might be able to emphasise with more force the relevance of her story today.

I also needed to find some way of conveying Seacole's heroism convincingly to an audience more sceptical of such a virtue now than it would have been a century and a half ago. Heroism has of course been the bread and butter of monuments through the ages, but the simpler notions of virtue and vice that characterised thinking in Seacole's time have been subjected over the past century to closer intellectual scrutiny. In the intervening period it has been borne in on us even more emphatically than before - not least by two world wars and the rise in psychoanalytic thinking - that we all have feet of clay and that our small graspings at courage and achievement are rooted in trepidation and doubt. In the kingdom of the psyche our shadow is always with us. Monuments celebrating raw human heroism are these days regularly treated as intellectually dubious or assumed no longer to be germane. It seemed to me that if I could literally give her shadow back to this heroic figure, I could undercut such doubts. By including a symbol of her ordinary fallible humanity, I could make her heroism all the more convincing.

So I conceived the idea of erecting behind the statue a fragment of the ground Seacole had herself once trod. Late in 2013 I travelled to Crimea to identify the original position of the British Hotel, the name she gave to the store and canteen she built close behind the army's lines south of Sevastopol. Small shards of broken glass, calcified by Crimean earth, lay scattered on the ground, remnants from the bottle store that had stood at the back of the long-vanished building. A short scramble from the site were the remains of a quarry that had been excavated during the same war to provide stone for the new supply route between Balaclava and the front. There is a deeply touching contemporaneous account of a young soldier terribly injured by an explosion in this quarry being carried over the field to die, not uncomforted on the stony ground as might ordinarily have been his fate, but in Mary Seacole's arms.

Accompanying me on the trip was a team from the foundry that would later cast the sculpture in bronze. We took an impression of a circular area of the quarry's rockface so we could set it up behind her statue. Buried now inside the bronze disc that replicates this rockface is a small piece of black glass from one of the shattered bottles that we found on the ground that day.

After sunset each evening her looming shadow will be thrown onto the rugged disc behind her by a spotlight. I like to think that when we now touch the disc we share for a moment in her history. Standing next to her figure after dusk, our own shadows will lengthen on the disc's surface, so that her battlefield will come to stand for our own.

History reaches forward from that war long ago towards our own time. Here and there on the Crimean hillside were rusting pieces of shrapnel from another battle fought on the same site a century later in World War II. On the quarry's rockface was the imprint of a shell blast from that war and it is visible now on the bronze disc. A short time after we returned, possession was taken of the whole of Crimea by Ukraine's neighbour. Some small corners of the earth seem forever destined to be battlefields. And not only literal ones, though standing this dusty fragment of a blood-soaked foreign land, like a big full-stop, immediately opposite the seat of our country's highest power, might make it seem very literal indeed.

Each monument that is raised changes the way we see ourselves. This statue shines with hope. It should be seen to mark not only the extraordinary courage of Mary Seacole herself but also the adventurousness, brilliance and generosity of black women like her throughout Britain. I have met those virtues in abundance in the course of making this sculpture. I hope the statue will add its small weight to a steady and irreversible shift in our nation's perception of itself, to increasing tolerance and understanding of each other, and to recognition that people coming to work in this country from abroad, not least in nursing, contribute far more to our nation than they cost it.

The battlefield is metaphorical and each of us has our own. There is a passage in her autobiography where Mary describes waiting in the hallway of the Secretary of State who had sent Florence Nightingale to the war. Mary is asking to join Nightingale's team. She sits listening to the minutes ticking by. Nobody comes to speak to her. Eventually she receives her chilly refusal. Later under a wintry dusk she wonders ruefully whether it is the colour of her skin that has elicited this contempt. She has been stonewalled. Not one of ours. Not there at all.

Mary turns her back on this stone wall. It is now part of her monument, a moment of pain cast in bronze. Undaunted, this battlefield nurse with the overflowing heart hitches up her skirts and marches into history. Treated as if she didn't belong, she has come to belong to us all.

Martin Jennings FRBS
Sculptor

Sir Hugh Taylor

MARY AND FLORENCE

By Sir Hugh Taylor

I am delighted that we are hosting this statue in memory of Mary Seacole in the gardens of St Thomas' Hospital. It is a fitting tribute to a remarkable woman, a person of courage and determination, committed to the service of others. But it goes further than that. Mary Seacole, and therefore her statue, could not be more relevant today. As she now stands proud – overlooking Parliament – she bears witness to what it means to be different in our society and the need to recognise it and honour it.

All of us who work in the NHS acknowledge the contribution that generations of healthcare workers from black and minority backgrounds have made to the NHS over the years. For them Mary Seacole is a pioneer, a role model for the courage and determination they have needed to follow their calling to serve their fellow human beings, often in challenging and sometimes hostile circumstances.

This statue stands for them as well as for her. For us here at Guy's and St Thomas' it speaks in a special way to the diversity of our local population, our patients and our staff – of which we are so proud.

I hope that the presence of a statue of this iconic figure in our gardens will serve as an inspiration to all our staff as they strive to provide high quality care to our patients.

One of our great challenges as a healthcare provider is to ensure that we are always restless to improve and to adapt our services to meet the needs of the communities that rely on us, to be there for them when they need us.

These needs change as the communities that we serve change and evolve over time – for example, we have pioneered specialist services to care for the large homeless population in our area, to support women who have suffered female genital mutilation

(FGM), and to meet the needs of people living with sickle cell disease.

Mary Seacole's legacy and her relevance to young people growing up in south London will be the focus of a new charity, the Mary Seacole Trust, now that the statue in her memory has been erected.

The Mary Seacole Trust's primary purpose will be educational and I am particularly pleased that it will be working closely with the Florence Nightingale Museum, which we are also proud to host at St Thomas'.

Some have attempted to drive a wedge between the legacies of Florence Nightingale and Mary Seacole. That is not our perspective. Florence Nightingale's personal association with St Thomas' is a matter of a deep pride to us. She is memorialised at the very heart of the hospital; and she will always have a special place in our hearts, for the contribution she made here – and, of course, much more widely – to hospital design, nurse education and training, and public health.

So we do not see the presence on our site of this signal of Mary Seacole's historic importance as in conflict with Florence Nightingale's legacy to this Trust, to the nursing profession, or to the nation. They are both remarkable figures in their own right - Victorian women, who in different ways and for different reasons, are still role models today.

The work of the Mary Seacole Trust, in partnership with the Florence Nightingale Museum, promises to celebrate their different legacies – not make point scoring comparisons - in line with the values we espouse as a Trust.

I would urge those with an interest in Mary Seacole to pay a visit to the Florence Nightingale Museum at St Thomas' which is full of interesting exhibits and information about Florence, as well as information about Mary Seacole, which it hopes to develop over time.

You can find out more at www.florence-nightingale.co.uk.

Sir Hugh Taylor
Chairman
Guy's and St Thomas' NHS Foundation Trust

Colonel DC Bates ARRC QHN BN MMedEd MPH FIHM FRSPH MIoD QARANC

ARMY PERSPECTIVES

By Colonel DC Bates ARRC QHN BN MMedEd MPH FIHM FRSPH MIoD QARANC

Mary Seacole was not an Army nurse, but neither was Florence Nightingale or any of the other British women operating in the Crimea Theatre of Operations (including Turkey) during that horrific conflict from 1854 to 56. Mary worked hard, like Nightingale, to improve the health and wellbeing of soldiers, making her own way to the front and becoming an integral part of the Allied military healthcare and welfare system in the Crimea. Moreover, she was not even a trained nurse, physician or surgeon in the classical sense but was a self-taught hybrid of apothecary, physician, nurse, surrogate mother (the soldiers' soubriquet) and of course entrepreneur[1]. It is perhaps the latter that drew criticism towards Mary's operation possibly seeing her through a jaundiced eye, but it can be argued that she was sustaining the moral component of fighting power, that inner will that keeps soldiers fighting, through both her treatment of the sick and wounded and by providing a facility where they could recuperate.

The Army Nursing Service was not set up until 1881, following Nightingale's recommendations, so the field hospitals were reliant on wives and a few orderlies drawn from the ranks to nurse or assist the Regimental Surgeons and their mates. The nascent Medical Staff Corps formed up in 1855 emulating the French model by providing 'men who could read and write, who were of regular habits and a kindly disposition' to work full time in the field hospitals[2].

But despite this innovation the British expeditionary force was still reliant on civilians like Mary Seacole, Florence Nightingale's team in Scutari, Eliza McKenzie leading the Royal

---

1   Robinson J (2005), Chapter 8 Proud and Unprotected. In Mary Seacole: The charismatic black nurse who became a heroine of the Crimea, pp 141. Constable and Robinson Limited.

2   http://www.army.mod.uk/medical-services/30000

Navy's mission in Sinope and Alexis Soyer who made improvements to hospital nutrition across the force. These people were all critical to delivering military effect and civilians still contribute to medicine and logistics on operations, what is now called 'the Whole Force Concept'.

Despite her critics, Mary Seacole's work was positively recognised by the people who mattered to her, the soldiers and officers who she called her sons. The Adjutant General, Lord William Paulet, praised Mary Seacole at the end of the war remembering her as an 'excellent woman' who 'frequently exerted herself in the most praiseworthy manner in attending wounded men, even in positions of great danger, and in assisting sick soldiers by all means in her power'. William Russell, Special Correspondent to *The Times*, praised her 'care under fire' and compassion when treating Allied or Russian casualties alike. He also observed her provision of primary healthcare at the 'British Hotel' praising her skill in successfully treating diarrhoea, dysentery and all sundry of camp ailments getting soldiers, navvies and the Land Transport men back to work quickly[3]. Indeed, the Inspector General of Hospitals in the East, Dr John Hall, sanctioned Mary Seacole's unsupervised practice of medicine in the Crimea, having personally inspected and approved her medicine chest[4]. This triangulation of testimonials would sit well in a 21st century nurse, doctor or medic's continuous professional development portfolio! This is the measure of the woman who is an inspiration for all health professionals operating in areas of conflict and catastrophe.

**Colonel DC Bates ARRC QHN BN MMedEd MPH FIHM FRSPH MIoD QARANC
Director, Army Nursing Services 2013 to 2016 and MSMSA Trustee since 2015**

---

3   Kerr P, Gold M, Cherfas T et al (1997), Chapter 5 Sisters of Mercy, in The Crimean War, pp 90.Boxtree, London.

4   Robinson J (2005), Chapter 8 Proud and Unprotected. In Mary Seacole: The charismatic black nurse who became a heroine of the Crimea, pp 142. Constable and Robinson Limited.

Lisa Rodrigues CBE

WHAT MARY SEACOLE MEANS TO ME

By Lisa Rodrigues CBE

I want to explain why I, a white woman, became an Ambassador for the Mary Seacole Memorial Statue Appeal in 2012, and why I have become a Trustee of the Mary Seacole Trust.

I started my NHS career as a nurse in a London teaching hospital in 1973. I was soon attracted to community services and through them, to mental health. I became involved in equality, diversity and human rights, and learned the impact that stigma and discrimination can have on patients, and also on staff.

When you work in the NHS, or when you become a patient, you notice immediately how many extraordinary healthcare professionals are black, Asian, mixed race or from other minority ethnic (BAME) backgrounds. In fact, 20% of all NHS staff are BAME, 30% of nurses and 40% of doctors. NHS staff are more ethnically diverse than the populations they serve. And yet, the situation for those in senior positions is rather different. Despite 70% of the NHS workforce being female, there appears to be a thick glass ceiling in the NHS for women. But there is an even thicker one for BAME people. Do you know how many NHS trust chief executives are BAME? Just one, out of 360. Which is shocking.

Young people entering NHS careers need role models. Otherwise, they invariably wonder whether their contribution is valued, and if leadership is really for them. So far, we haven't done well enough in the NHS, although we keep saying we want to which brings me to Mary Seacole. Mary was a mixed race woman who had a distinguished international healthcare career before she applied to go to the Crimean War to nurse wounded and dying British soldiers. And yet, despite all that she did and sacrificed, her important place in our military and NHS history has not been properly recognised or used to benefit people who experience discrimination. Until now.

Mary's statue can help to change that. Mary's legacy will be to show young people of all ethnic backgrounds that skill and compassion, combined with application and determination, are the essential ingredients for success. She will demonstrate that people like her, women and those from BAME backgrounds, can succeed if they work hard, confront resistance, are given support and never give up hope.

I hope you will visit the statue and stop to marvel at what one steadfast, courageous, entrepreneurial woman did 160 years ago. And please listen out for more news about the Mary Seacole Trust – with our new chair Trevor Sterling, we intend to be a force for positive change.

Lisa Rodrigues CBE
Trustee, Mary Seacole Trust

Mrs. Diedre Mills

A PIONEERING JAMAICAN

By Mrs. Diedre Mills

For Jamaicans, Mary Seacole is recognised and remembered as a trailblazer.

She is indeed among the many pioneering Jamaicans whose work and accomplishments have ensured that our small island in the Caribbean is recognised positively throughout the world.

At a time when it was not the norm, and it was in fact frowned upon for a woman, especially a woman of colour, to travel alone, Mary Seacole defied the convention of the day and not only travelled to the 'motherland' but also to the battlefields of the Crimean War.

Her experience treating patients in the cholera epidemic of 1850 – 1851 in Jamaica and Panama resulted in her being asked by the Jamaican medical authorities in 1853 to minister to victims of a severe outbreak of yellow fever. These experiences enabled her to not only hone her skills but also prepared her for the monumental task that would face her in Crimea.

She is fondly remembered in Jamaica for her care of those who were ailing, including those who were not able to pay for her services.

Her generosity of heart and spirit resulted in her being posthumously awarded the fourth-highest honour in Jamaica in 1991 - the Order of Merit. In recognition of her sterling contribution to the medical field, the headquarters of the Nurses' Association of Jamaica in Kingston was named "Mary Seacole House" in 1954, and a hall of residence at the University of the West Indies in Mona, Jamaica, still bears her name.

Mary Seacole made her mark on both Jamaican and British history as a woman of compassion, determination, discipline, character and courage. She has been an inspiration to many generations of Jamaicans at home and in the Diaspora. It comes as no surprise, therefore, that she was declared the greatest Black Briton in a poll conducted in 2004. We continue to be inspired by her great achievements and are proud to claim her as one of our own.

Mrs. Diedre Mills
Deputy (Acting High) Commissioner, Jamaican High Commission, United Kingdom

PERSONAL WARMTH

For me it was a great thrill to get involved in the appeal for Mary Seacole's statue. One of the reasons of course is how few black women have been remembered in this way. It was especially important to remember a woman who was in Crimea. I love the fact that her personal warmth made her such a favourite with the soldiers so that they could relax and enjoy themselves.

Shreela Flather
Baroness Flather JP DL FRSA
MSMSA Trustee

MARY
SEACOLE
MEMORIAL STATUE APPEAL

FIVE-YEAR MISSION

Little did I know that the words "How can someone help?" would be the beginning of a five-year mission to see the memorial statue of Mary Seacole erected in the gardens of St Thomas' Hospital, facing the Houses of Parliament.

Not unlike Mary, the Appeal has faced many obstacles, each one a stepping stone to achieving a shared vision. This statue is a true reflection of Mary's resilience, character, sense of purpose and adventure.

"and the grateful words and smile which rewarded me for binding up a wound or giving a cooling drink was a pleasure worth risking life for at any time."
Mary Seacole
Wonderful Adventures of Mrs Seacole in Many Lands

Roxanne St. Clair
MSMSA Trustee (Treasurer/Project Manager)

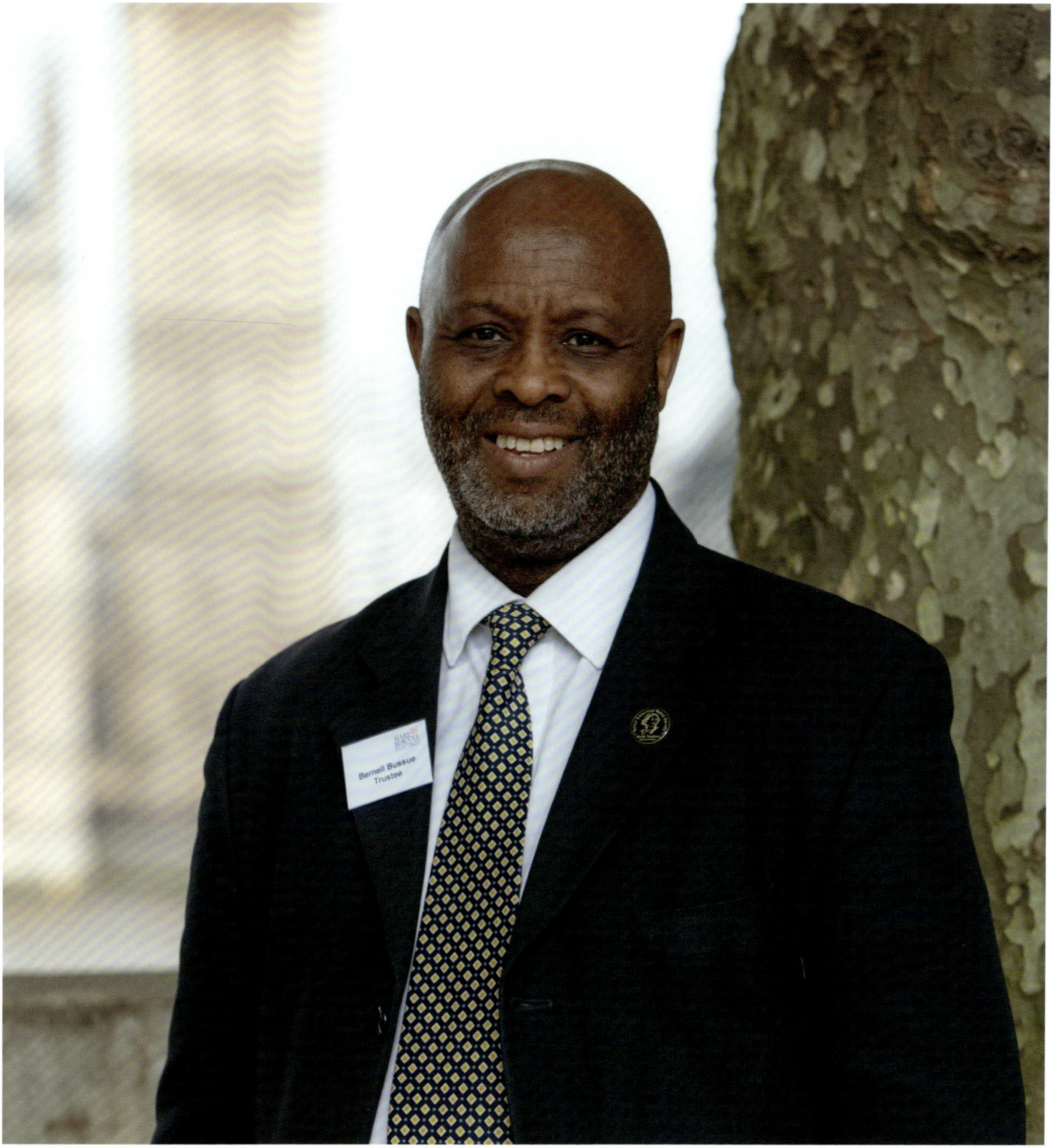
Bernell Bussue
Trustee

ERASED FROM HISTORY

My interest in Mary Seacole started when I bought the 1984 edition of her autobiography, *Wonderful Adventures of Mrs Seacole in Many Lands*, edited by Ziggi Alexander and Audrey Dewjee, at a Mary Seacole Memorial Association annual meeting held at the Jamaican High Commission in London.

I was struck by how such a remarkable woman had faded from history and vowed to see what I could do in my sphere of influence to secure change. Around the same period, I was privileged to become a member of the Mary Seacole Awards steering committee where on behalf of the Royal College of Nursing I reviewed applications, assessed the suitability of their proposals and supported recipients of the awards. Projects had to focus on areas likely to improve health outcomes of people from black and minority ethnic communities. Through these opportunities, I learned even more about Mary and had my personal viewpoint reinforced, and that is that racism played a clear part in Mary being erased from history.

Later, when I was invited by Professor Elizabeth Anionwu to join the Mary Seacole Memorial Statue Appeal, I was pleased to take on the role of Trustee and was delighted to witness the unveiling of Mary's statue at St Thomas' Hospital on 30 June 2016. The long fundraising journey with fellow Trustees bears some of the hallmarks of Mary's struggle against, and triumphs over, adversity. I trust what I brought to the committee was to be a good team player, diplomacy skills, the ability to provide a bridge between different groups and networks plus a tenacity and desire to see something through to completion. However, what I gained from the experiences and the friendships made is way more than I could have contributed, which I truly appreciate.

Bernell Bussue
MSMSA Trustee

MARY
SEACOLE
MEMORIAL
STATUE APPEAL

MY INSPIRATION

I became aware of Mary Seacole as a young girl attending black history study classes. I am extremely proud that Mary was born in Kingston, Jamaica, the same place as my mother. Mary is an inspiration to me. She showed a tremendous amount of courage to overcome barriers of racial discrimination to achieve her ambition of nursing the wounded soldiers in Crimea, as well as being an entrepreneur to finance her medical and nursing practice.

Georgina Osbourne
MSMSA Trustee

MARY
SEACOLE
MEMORIAL
STATUE APPEAL

WHAT IT MEANS TO BE GREAT

This is a fantastic tribute to our 'great black Briton'. Not only was she an inspirational role model but a courageous and passionate woman who put others before herself - a true testament of what it is to be Great!

Marsha John-Greenwood
MSMSA Trustee

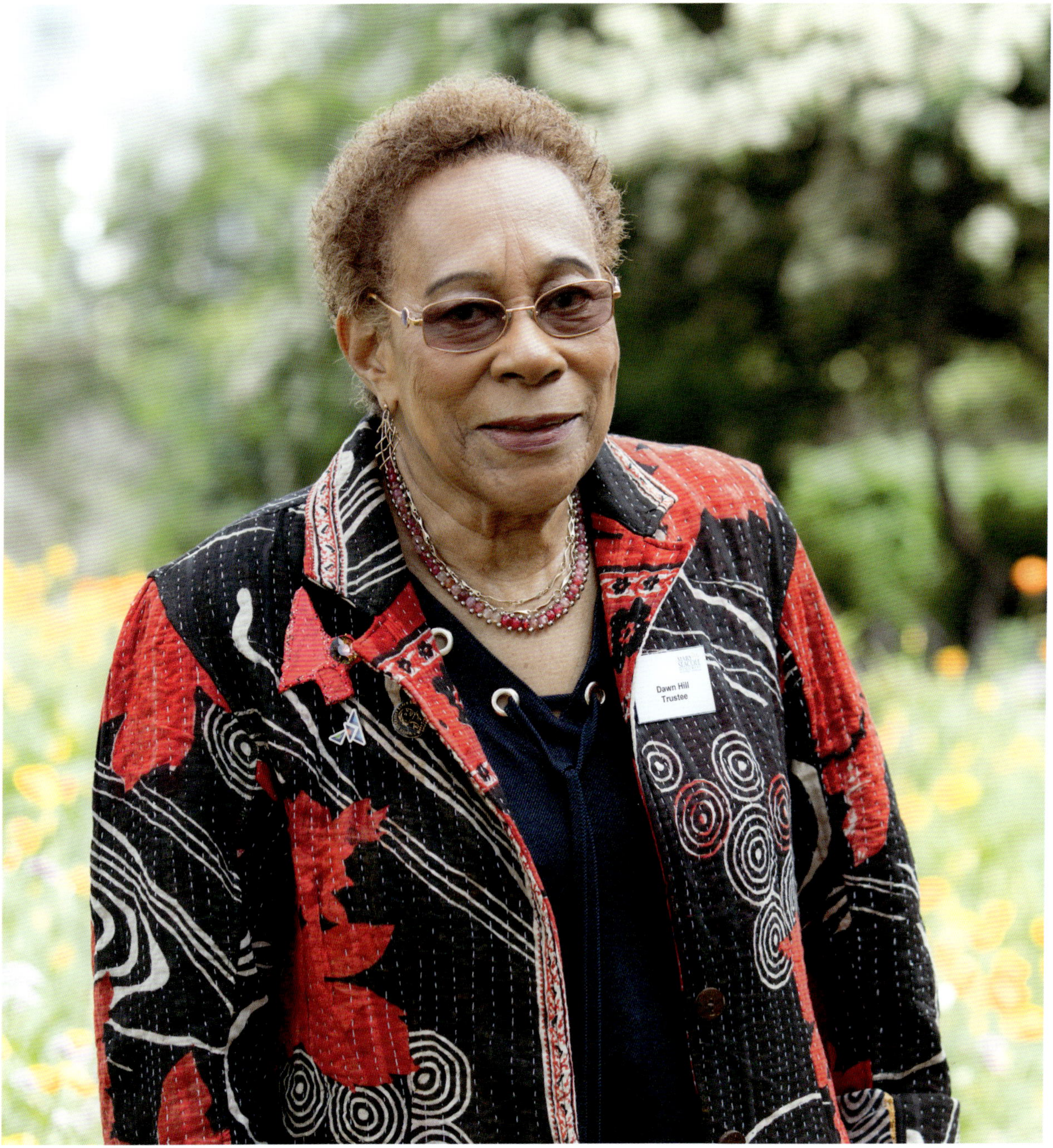
Dawn Hill
Trustee

HISTORIC ACHIEVEMENT

Black Cultural Archives congratulates the historic achievement of the MSMSA and is proud to support its legacy Mary Seacole Trust.

Dawn Hill
Chairman, Black Cultural Archives
Member of Guys and St Thomas' NHS Foundation Trust

Dawn is the MSMSA Trustee who led the team responsible for organising the unvieling.

MARY
SEACOLE
MEMORIAL
STATUE APPEAL

MOVING JUSTGIVING TRIBUTES

I became involved with the Mary Seacole Memorial Statue Appeal by accident. I was working at Essentia, the infrastructure directorate of Guy's and St Thomas' NHS Foundation Trust, and was invited to help with fundraising for the Last Lap of the campaign. I had heard of Mary Seacole from my children who studied her at school, but I knew very little about her.

What began as a work project, however, quickly turned into a deeper personal commitment. I learned more about this amazing woman who achieved extraordinary things and showed great determination and resilience in doing so. But what really moved me were the comments on the Appeal's JustGiving site, from the hundreds of ordinary people who said how important and inspirational Mary has been in their lives. She stood for fairness and equality and inclusion. Her statue will stand tall and inspire many more people and I feel very privileged to have been involved.

Tracy Cheung

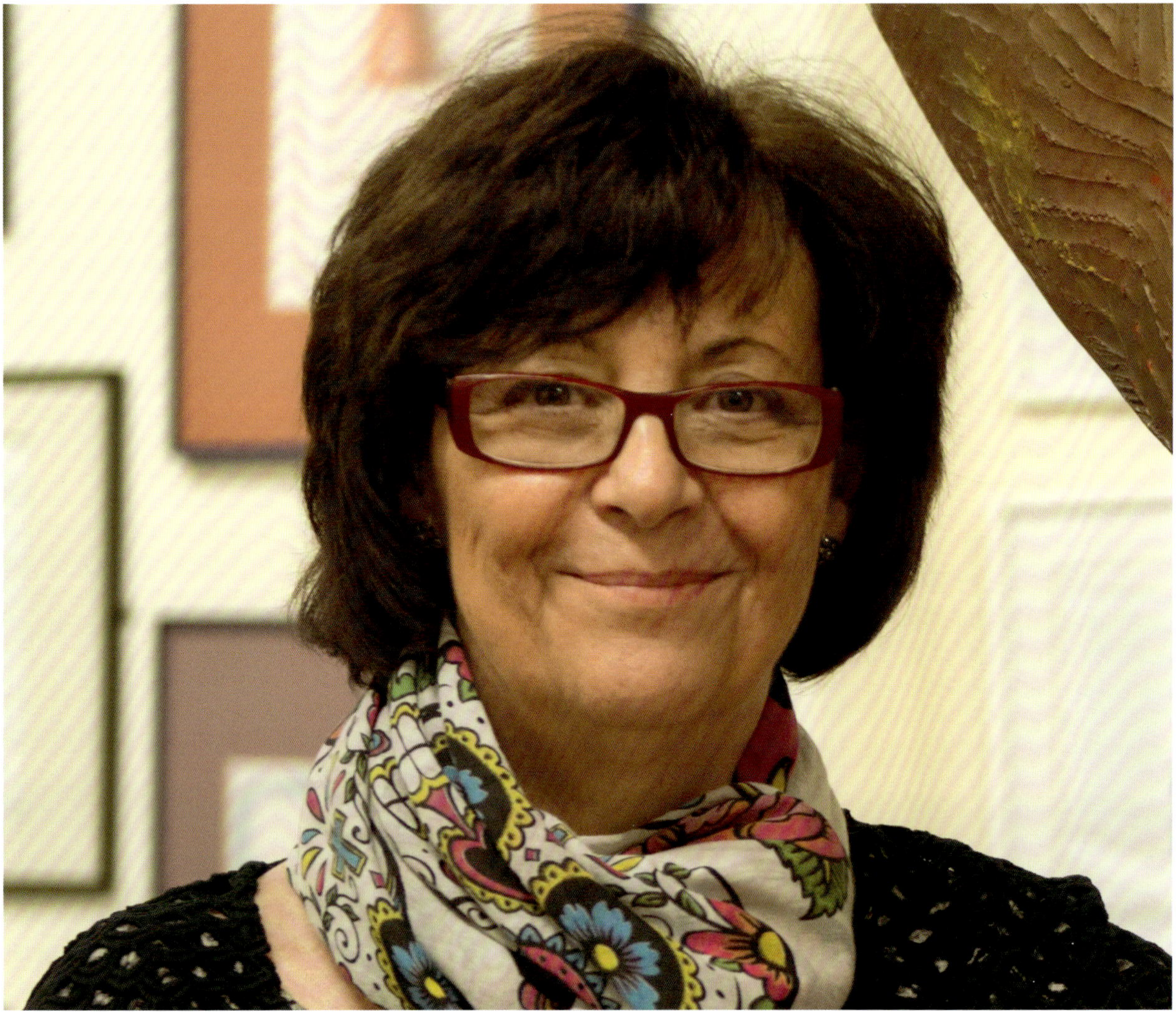

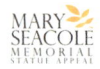

ADMIRED AND APPLAUDED

It has been a pleasure to sponsor the Appeal and to enable, as best we may, this wonderful memorial to the intrepid figure of Mary Seacole. As both nurse and brave entrepreneur, Mary represents for us a woman to be admired and applauded.

Philomena Davidson PPRBS RWA, Independent arts consultant and Director of the Davidson Arts Project; and her daughter Lucy Davis, Director of DAP Creative

MARY
SEACOLE
MEMORIAL STATUE APPEAL

FUTURE LEGACY

I am proud to have worked with the Mary Seacole Memorial Statue Appeal and to share the seismic work of the trustees, ambassadors and supporters determined to ensure Mary finally receives the recognition she deserves.

The statue of Mary Seacole will not only serve as a lasting memorial but will also be a valuable opportunity to remind the British public of her values and sacrifices. It will act as a celebration of the UK's diversity, providing much needed acknowledgement of the contribution black, Asian and ethnic minorities have made throughout British history.

It is to be my privilege to hold the position of Chair of the Mary Seacole Trust, the new guise of the Mary Seacole Memorial Statue Appeal, which will emerge following the unveiling of the statue. The Trust will have the honour of shaping and delivering a legacy beyond the wonderful statue itself.

The Mary Seacole Trust will endeavour to educate the public and increase awareness of Mary Seacole, advancing her value as a role model in order to inspire and promote good citizenship, particularly with young people.

Amongst other things, the Trust will strive for recognition of achievers within public and private sector organisations, with the aim of promoting diversity in leadership and equality of outcomes.

The Wonderful Adventures of Mrs Seacole continue and long may they do so…

Trevor Sterling, Chair, Mary Seacole Trust

MARY
SEACOLE
MEMORIAL
STATUE APPEAL

PATRONS

President of the Royal College of Nursing

Mayor of London

The High Commissioner for Jamaica

President of the Trades Union Congress

General Secretary of Unite

President of UNISON

Chair of the Equality and Human Rights Commission

The Rt. Hon. the Baroness Dean of Thornton-le-Fylde

The Rt. Hon. the Lord Luce KG GCVO DL

The Rt. Hon. Lord Selkirk of Douglas QC

The Viscount Slim OBE DL

TRUSTEES Pg 57-60

Lord Soley, Professor Elizabeth Anionwu CBE FRCN, Roxanne St Clair, Juliet Alexander, Colonel David Bates ARRC L/QARANC, Bernell Bussue, Baroness Flather JP DL FRSA, Celia Grandison-Markey, Dawn Hill, Maxine Hurley, Marsha John-Greenwood, Professor Dr Zenobia Nadirshaw, Gina Osbourne, Lisa Rodrigues CBE, Trevor Sterling

SECRETARY Pg 61

Steve Marsh

MEDIA ADVISER Pg 61

Jean Gray

AMBASSADORS Pg 62-71

Gail Adams, obi amadi, Alexander Amosu, Charmagne Barnes, Malorie Blackman OBE, Yinglen Butt, Tim Campbell MBE, Dr Geoffrey Day, Colonel A P Finnegan PhD L/QARANC, Rodney Hinds, Susan Howkins, Judith Jacob, Paul Jebb, Ms Stacy Johnson, Felicia Kwaku, Joan Pons Laplana, Denise Lewis OBE, Mr Rudi Lickwood, Leon Mann, Gloria Mills CBE, Joan Myers OBE, Suzanne Packer, Adriana Paice, Professor Sir Geoff Palmer OBE, Courtney Pine CBE, Michael Rosen, Joan Saddler OBE, Tom Sandford, Mr & Mrs Noel Seacole, Maggie Semple OBE, Professor Laura Serrant, Josette Simon OBE, Eleanor Smith, Doctors Corry and Jeroen Staring-Derks, Cleo Sylvestre, Rudolph Walker OBE, Jackie Weatherill, Sir Willard White OM CBE

TRUSTEE
CHAIR
LORD SOLEY OF HAMMERSMITH

TRUSTEE
VICE CHAIR
PROFESSOR ELIZABETH ANIONWU CBE FRCN

TRUSTEE
TREASURER
ROXANNE ST CLAIR

TRUSTEE
JULIET ALEXANDER

TRUSTEE
COLONEL DAVID BATES ARRC L/QARANC

TRUSTEE
BERNELL BUSSUE

TRUSTEE
BARONESS FLATHER JP DL FRSA

TRUSTEE
CELIA GRANDISON-MARKEY

TRUSTEE
DAWN HILL

TRUSTEE
MAXINE HURLEY

TRUSTEE
MARSHA JOHN-GREENWOOD

TRUSTEE
PROFESSOR DR ZENOBIA NADIRSHAW

TRUSTEE
GINA OSBOURNE

TRUSTEE
LISA RODRIGUES CBE

TRUSTEE
TREVOR STERLING

SECRETARY
STEVE MARSH

MEDIA ADVISER
JEAN GRAY

AMBASSADOR
HEAD OF NURSING, UNISON
GAIL ADAMS

AMBASSADOR
LEAD PROFESSIONAL OFFICER FOR THE TRADE UNION UNITE/CPHVA (COMMUNITY PRACTITIONERS' & HEALTH VISITORS' ASSOCIATION)
OBI AMADI

AMBASSADOR
BUSINESS ENTREPENEUR
ALEXANDER AMOSU

AMBASSADOR
DEAN, COLLEGE OF NURSING, MIDWIFERY AND HEALTHCARE, UNIVERSITY OF WEST LONDON
CHARMAGNE BARNES

AMBASSADOR
AWARD WINNING CHILDREN'S AUTHOR AND
CHILDREN'S LAUREATE: 2013-2015
MALORIE BLACKMAN OBE

AMBASSADOR
FORMER DEPUTY CHIEF NURSE/COMMUNITY,
GUY'S & ST THOMAS' NHS FOUNDATION TRUST
YINGLEN BUTT

AMBASSADOR
ENTREPRENEUR AND WINNER OF BBC2 'THE
APPRENTICE'
TIM CAMPBELL MBE

AMBASSADOR
FELLOWS' & ECCLES LIBRARIAN, WINCHESTER
COLLEGE
DR GEOFFREY DAY

AMBASSADOR
PROFESSOR OF NURSING AND HEAD OF THE
ACADEMIC DEPARTMENT OF MILITARY NURSING,
ROYAL CENTRE FOR DEFENCE MEDICINE,
BIRMINGHAM
COLONEL A P FINNEGAN PHD L/QARANC

AMBASSADOR
SPORTS AND FEATURES EDITOR, THE VOICE
NEWSPAPER
RODNEY HINDS

AMBASSADOR
ROYAL COLLEGE OF NURSING LONDON BOARD
MEMBER, INNER NORTH WEST LONDON
SUSAN HOWKINS

AMBASSADOR
ACTOR
JUDITH JACOB

AMBASSADOR
EXPERIENCE OF CARE PROFESSIONAL LEAD,
NHS ENGLAND (SECONDMENT FROM POST
OF ASSISTANT DIRECTOR OF NURSING PATIENT
EXPERIENCE, BLACKPOOL TEACHING HOSPITALS NHS
FOUNDATION TRUST)
PAUL JEBB

AMBASSADOR
LECTURER, UNIVERSITY OF NOTTINGHAM
SCHOOL OF HEALTH SCIENCES
MS STACY JOHNSON

AMBASSADOR
DEPUTY CHAIR OF THE CNO BME ADVISORY
GROUP
FELICIA KWAKU

AMBASSADOR
NHS NURSE CAREMAKER
JOAN PONS LAPLANA

AMBASSADOR
FORMER OLYMPIC GOLD MEDALLIST
AND BROADCASTER
DENISE LEWIS OBE

AMBASSADOR
COMEDIAN
MR RUDI LICKWOOD

AMBASSADOR
BBC AND ITV BROADCASTER AND FILM-MAKER
LEON MANN

AMBASSADOR
NATIONAL SECRETARY EQUALITIES, UNISON
GLORIA MILLS CBE

AMBASSADOR
CHILD NURSE CONSULTANT
AND CHAIR OF THE CNO BME ADVISORY GROUP
JOAN MYERS OBE

AMBASSADOR
ACTRESS
SUZANNE PACKER

AMBASSADOR
ARTIST AND CURATOR
ADRIANA PAICE

AMBASSADOR
PROFESSOR EMERITUS, SCHOOL OF LIFE
SCIENCES, HERIOT-WATT UNIVERSITY IN
EDINBURGH
PROFESSOR SIR GEOFF PALMER OBE

AMBASSADOR
JAZZ MUSICIAN
COURTNEY PINE CBE

AMBASSADOR
WRITER AND BROADCASTER
MICHAEL ROSEN

AMBASSADOR
ASSOCIATE DIRECTOR OF PATIENTS AND
COMMUNITIES, NHS CONFEDERATION
JOAN SADDLER OBE

AMBASSADOR
EXECUTIVE DIRECTOR, ROYAL COLLEGE OF
NURSING
TOM SANDFORD

AMBASSADOR
SEACOLE FAMILY
MR & MRS NOEL SEACOLE

AMBASSADOR
CHIEF EXECUTIVE OFFICER, THE EXPERIENCE
CORPS
MAGGIE SEMPLE OBE

AMBASSADOR
PROFESSOR LAURA SERRANT

AMBASSADOR
ACTOR
JOSETTE SIMON OBE

AMBASSADOR
THEATRE NURSE, BIRMINGHAM WOMEN'S NHS HOSPITAL. ELECTED UNISON'S FIRST BLACK PRESIDENT, 2012
ELEANOR SMITH

AMBASSADOR
MARY SEACOLE RESEARCHERS
DOCTORS CORRY AND JEROEN STARING-DERKS

AMBASSADOR
ACTOR
CLEO SYLVESTRE

AMBASSADOR
ACTOR
RUDOLPH WALKER OBE

AMBASSADOR
MARY SEACOLE FILM PRODUCER
JACKIE WEATHERILL

AMBASSADOR
OPERA SINGER
SIR WILLARD WHITE OM CBE

MARY
SEACOLE
MEMORIAL
STATUE APPEAL

COMMUNITY FUNDRAISING

Two fundraising strands developed to finance the statue.

Chairman Lord Clive Soley focused on securing significant donations from business, philanthropists and grant-making bodies while Vice Chairperson, Professor Elizabeth Anionwu, led on community fundraising with organisations including trade unions, professional associations, community groups and schools.

Facebook and Twitter accounts were created and Online donations enabled through a JustGiving site and a successful £80,000 'LastLap' campaign.

Over 40 Appeal Ambassadors helped to organise and took part in events, including:

- 'Laugh with Mary', sponsored by Unison and Black Cat Productions, organised by Ambassador and comedian Rudi Lickwood, featuring stars such as Jo Brand, Nathan Caton and Omid Djalili
- Jazz concerts headed up by saxophonist supremo Dr Courtney Pine CBE
- An 'Evening with Malorie Blackman OBE', bestselling author and past Children's Laureate
- Joan Saddler OBE organised a Red Carpet Evening and a stunning London Adventist Chorale Gospel Concert
- House of Lords teas were organised by Joan Myers OBE
- There were personal endeavours such as Paul Jebb's sponsored bike ride and Joan Pons Laplana's marathon run

Free stands were provided at conferences by organisations such as Unison, the Royal College of Nursing, Unite, NHS Confederation, NHS Employers, Chief Nursing Officer – NHS England and many NHS Trusts.

We were touched by the stream of donations from anonymous individuals. Our thanks to everyone – this was a wonderful example of crowdfunding, even before the term became popular!

The photographs that follow show just some of the many events that helped raise funds.

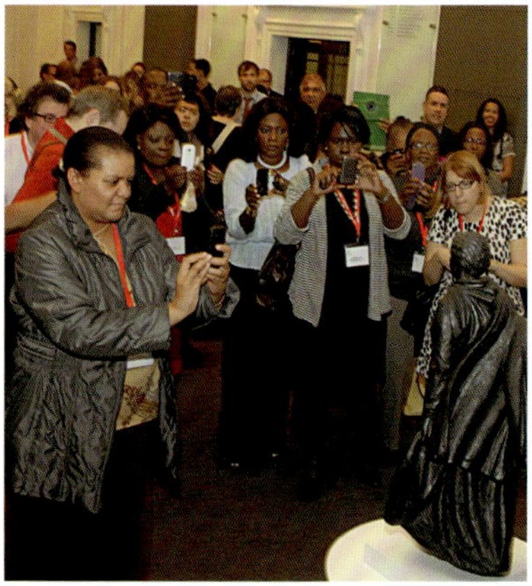

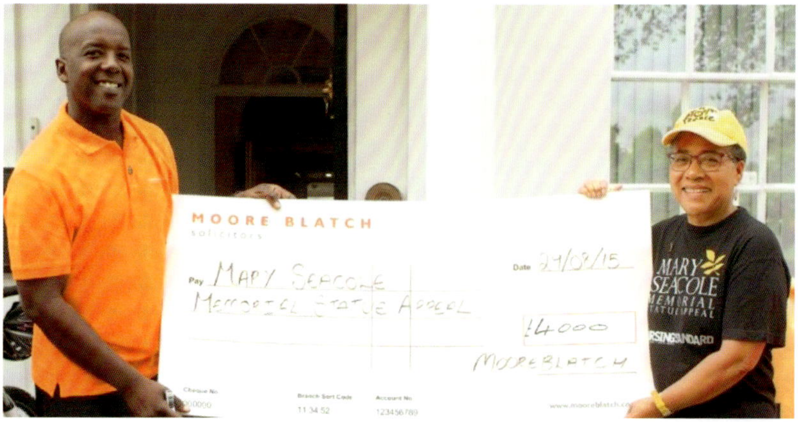

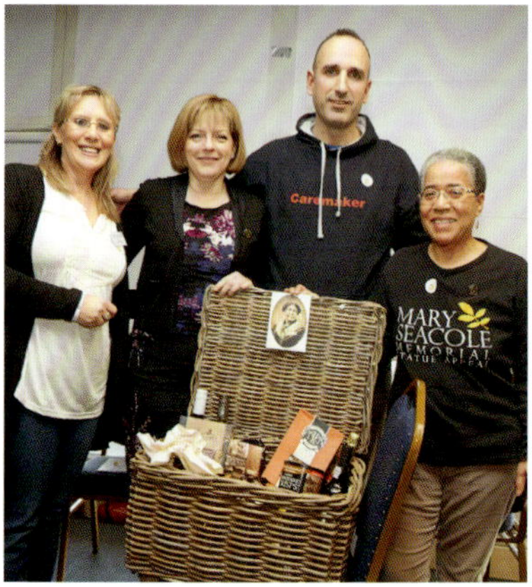

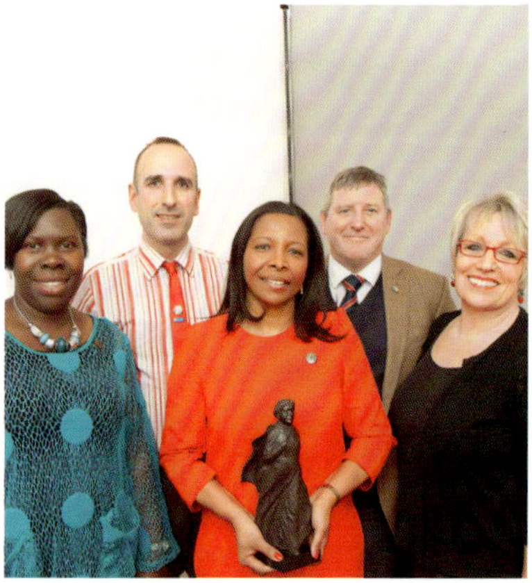

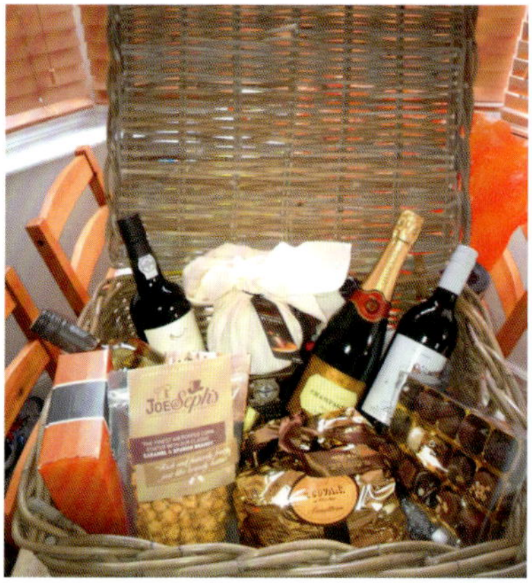

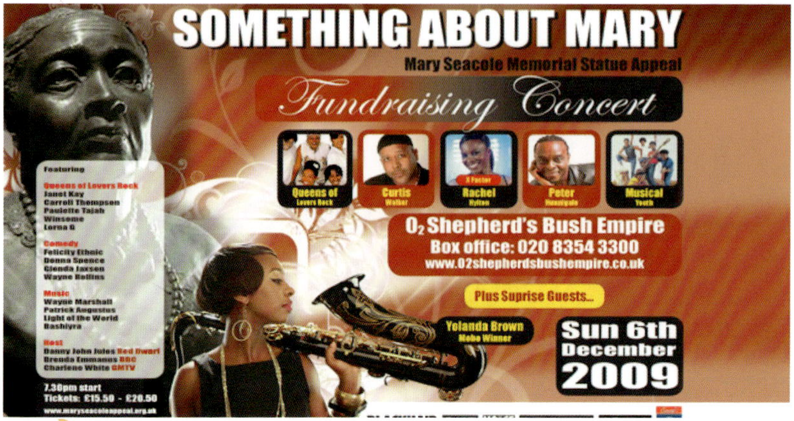

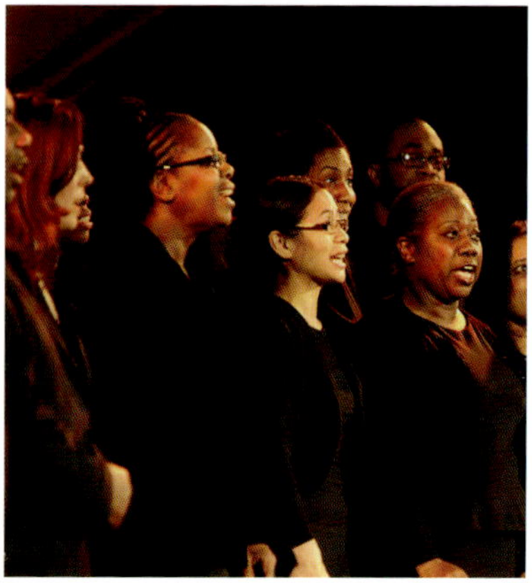

MARY SEACOLE MEMORIAL STATUE APPEAL

75

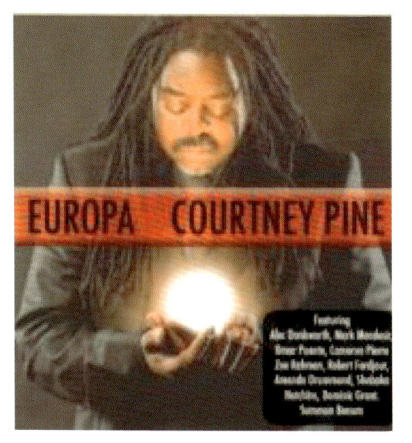

MARY
SEACOLE
MEMORIAL
STATUE APPEAL

THE MAKING OF THE SCULPTURE

To make the disc that would stand behind the statue of Mary Seacole, Martin Jennings travelled to Crimea with Rungwe Kingdon and Joe Carpenter from Pangolin Editions, the bronze foundry that would cast both elements. Consulting old maps from the mid-19th century to identify the site of Mary's base they took a digital scan of the neighbouring rockface. Back at the foundry, the image was compressed and 3D-printed as a 4.5m diameter circle before sand-casting in bronze and patinating a dusty grey.

Meanwhile Jennings modelled the full-size statue of Mary 3m high in clay on a steel armature, having gradually scaled it up from one-tenth and one-quarter scale maquettes. Pangolin took a rubber mould of the finished work from which the sections of the statue were cast in bronze before being welded together, metalworked and patinated. Jennings joined forces with stonecarver Danny Evans to cut the statue's inscriptions in Cumbrian slate and finally the day came when all the elements could be transported to site for installation. With a finished weight of 1.5 tons for the figure of Mary and more than 5 tons for the disc, this was no mean task. Late one evening in June 2016 the statue of Mary Seacole and the bronze impression of her 160 year-old battlefield were finally lowered into position by the banks of the Thames. By the end of the month a remarkable combination of historical research, digital and traditional craftsmanship, art, engineering and landscaping had come together and a new monument had taken its place in the capital city.

With special thanks to Rungwe Kingdon, Claude Koenig and Steve Maule of Pangolin Editions

IN CRIMEA

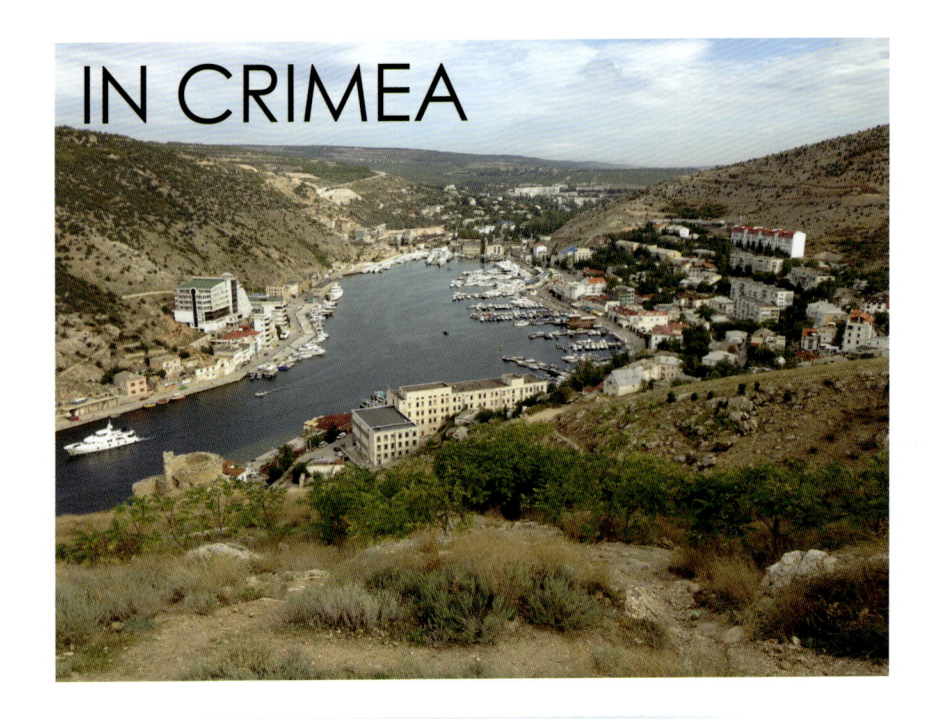

Rungwe Kingdon and Joe Carpenter from Pangolin Editions scan the rockface in Crimea

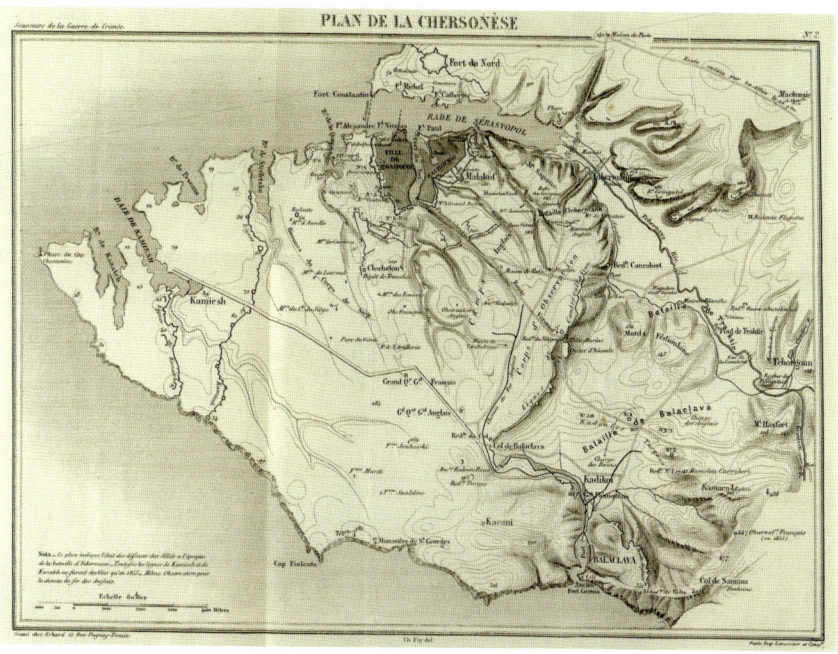

Old maps from the mid-19th century to identify the site of Mary's base

IN THE STUDIO

MARY SEACOLE
Pioneer Nurse

MARY SEACOLE
MEMORIAL
STATUE APPEAL

81

AT THE FOUNDRY

83

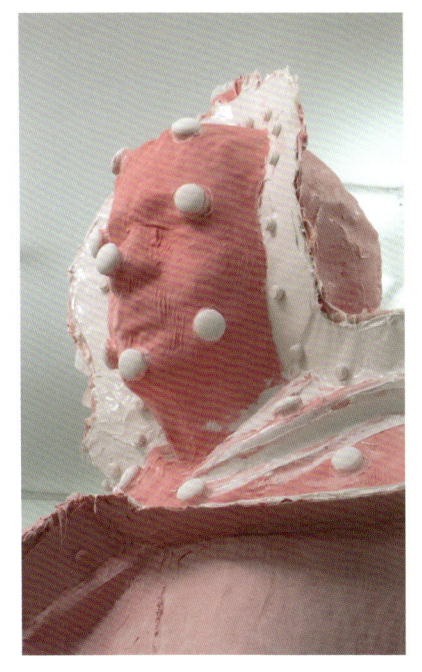

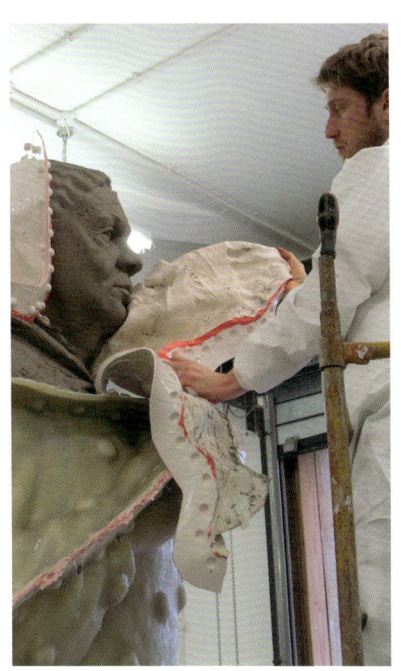

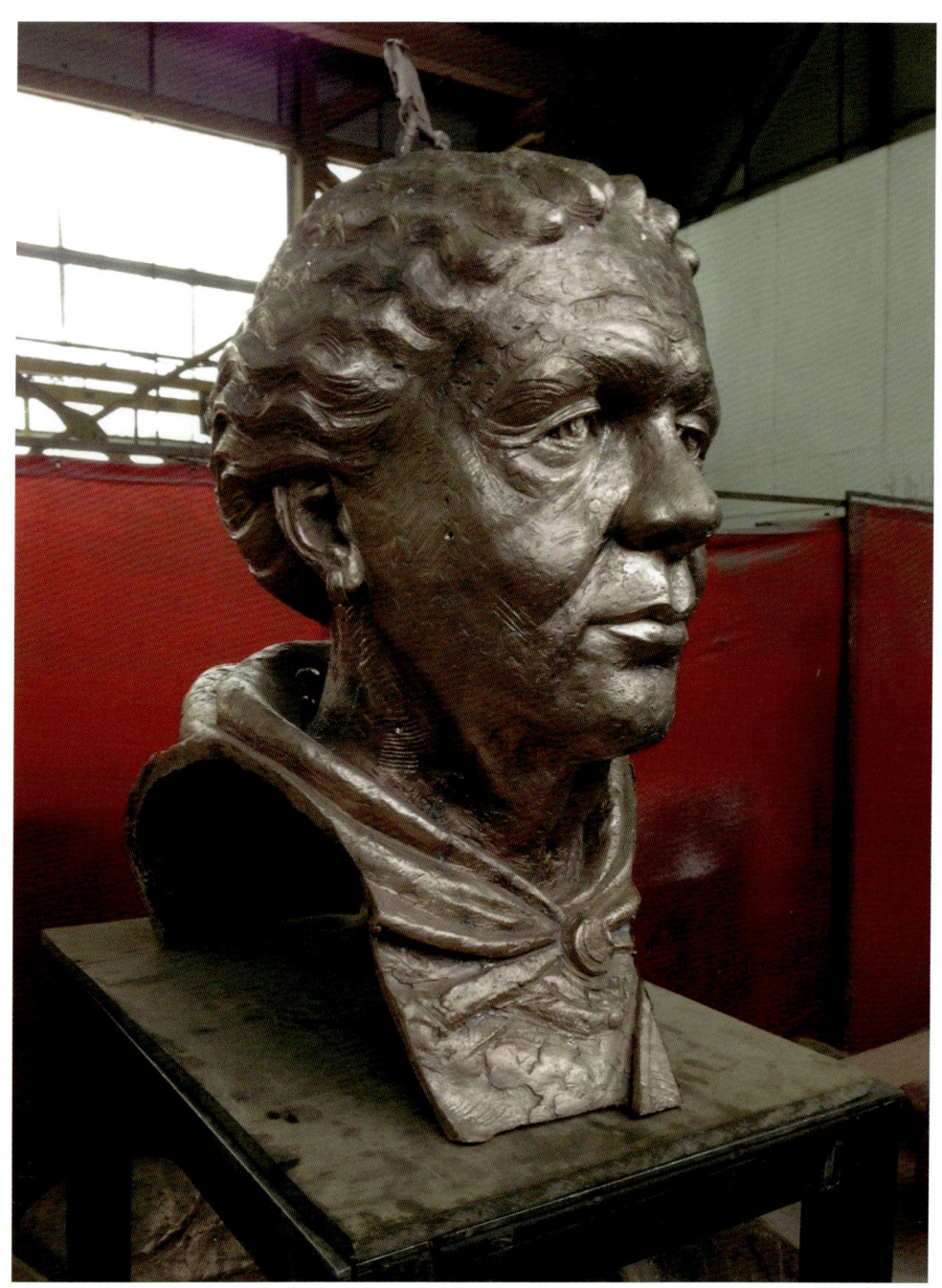

MARY
SEACOLE
MEMORIAL
STATUE APPEAL

85

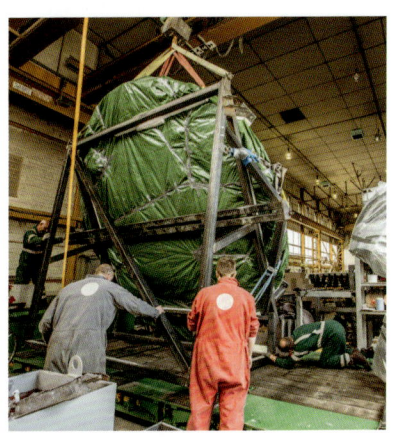

MARY
SEACOLE
MEMORIAL
STATUE APPEAL

87

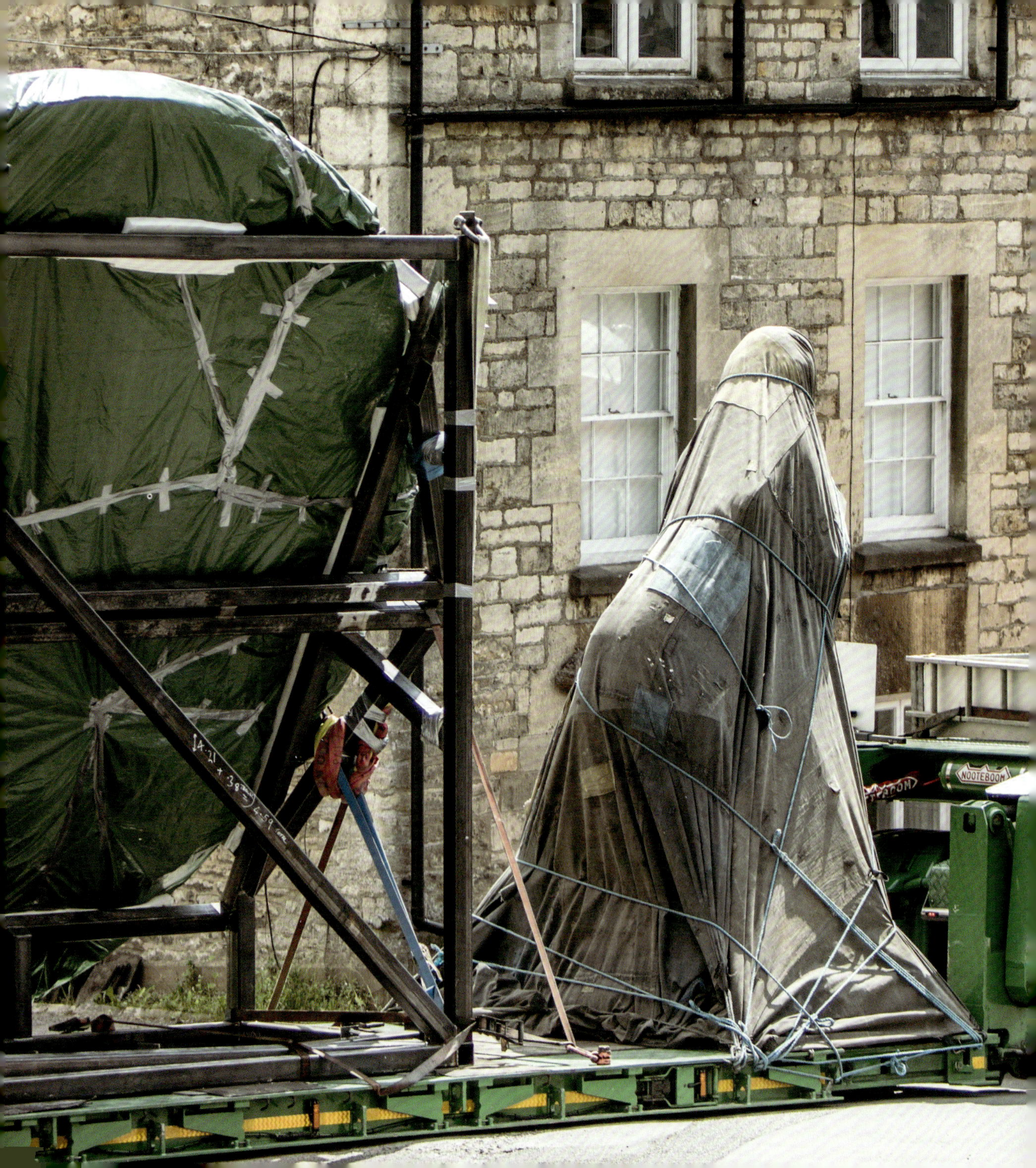
NOOTEBOOM

Quality in motion
www.russell-transport.com
CONVOI EXCEPTIONNEL
RUSSELL TRANSPORT
Cheltenham UK
Tel: +44 (0)1242 680378
NOOTEBOOM
RUSSELL TRANSPORT
01242
680378
CHELTENHAM
ENGLAND
SCANIA
SCANIA

INSTALLATION

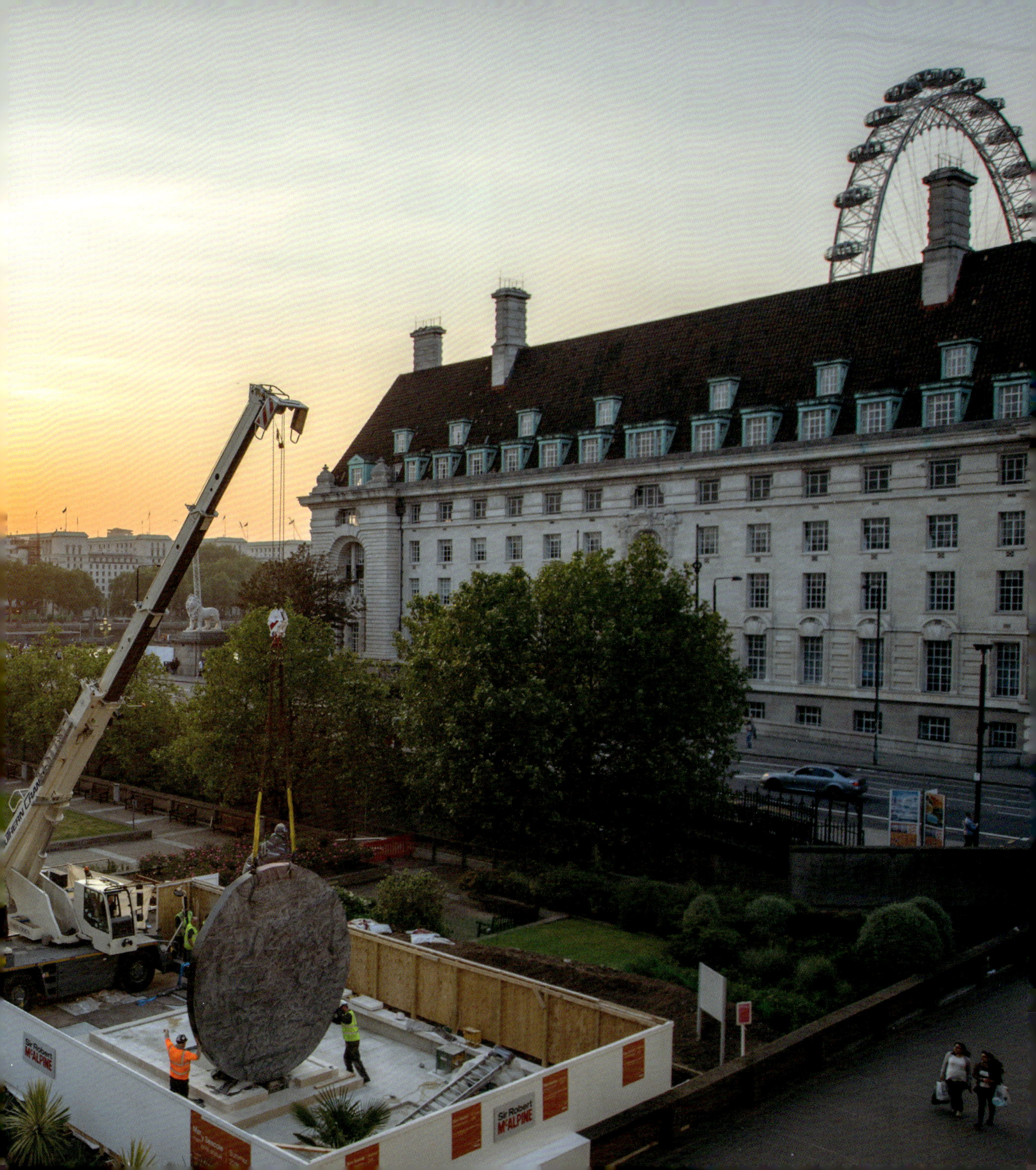

Sir Robert
McALPINE
Sir Robert
McALPINE

MARY
SEACOLE
MEMORIAL
STATUE APPEAL

93

MARY
SEACOLE
MEMORIAL
STATUE APPEAL

95

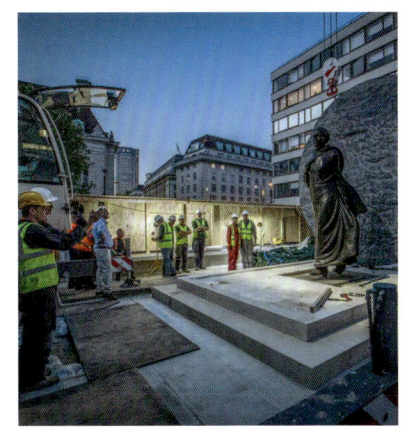

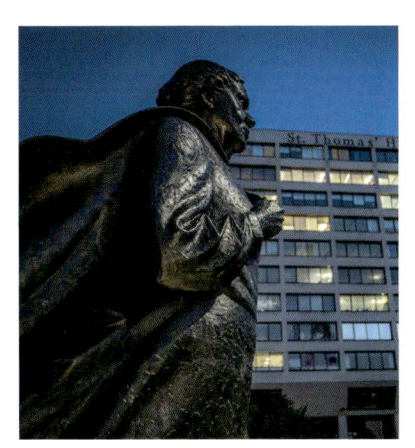

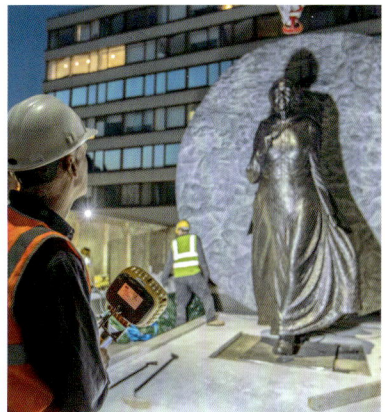

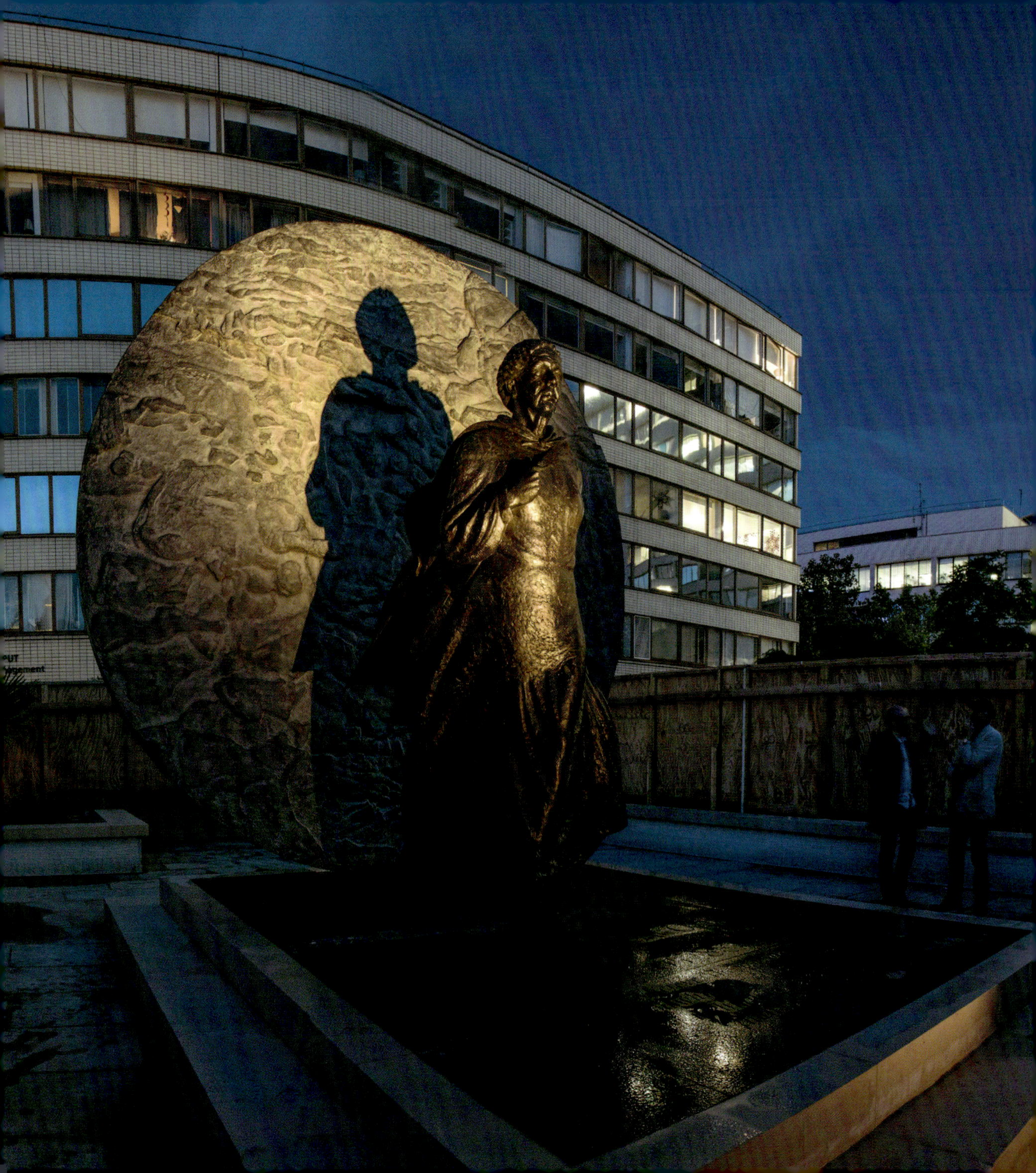

LIGHTING TESTS

MARY
SEACOLE
MEMORIAL
STATUE APPEAL

99

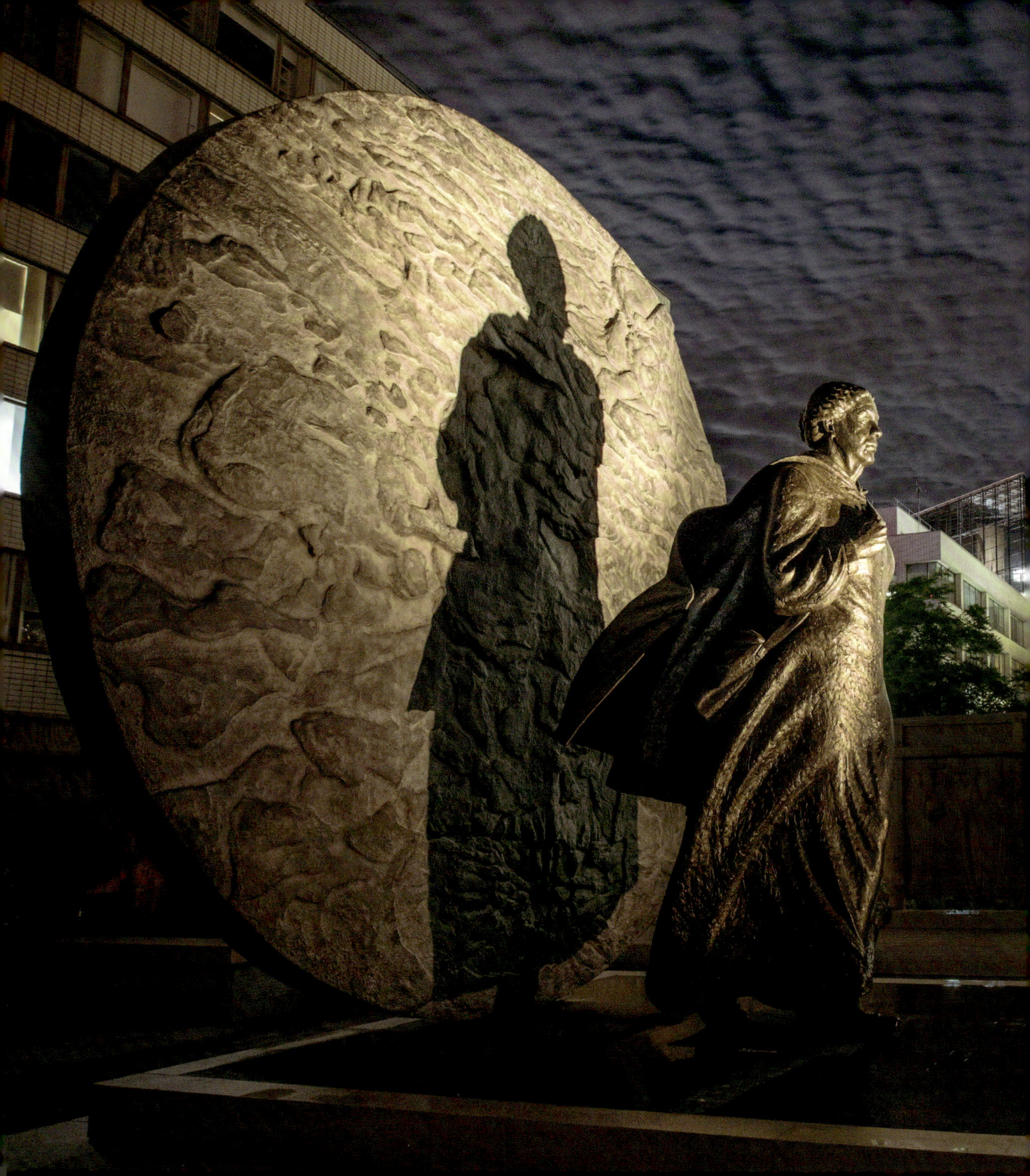

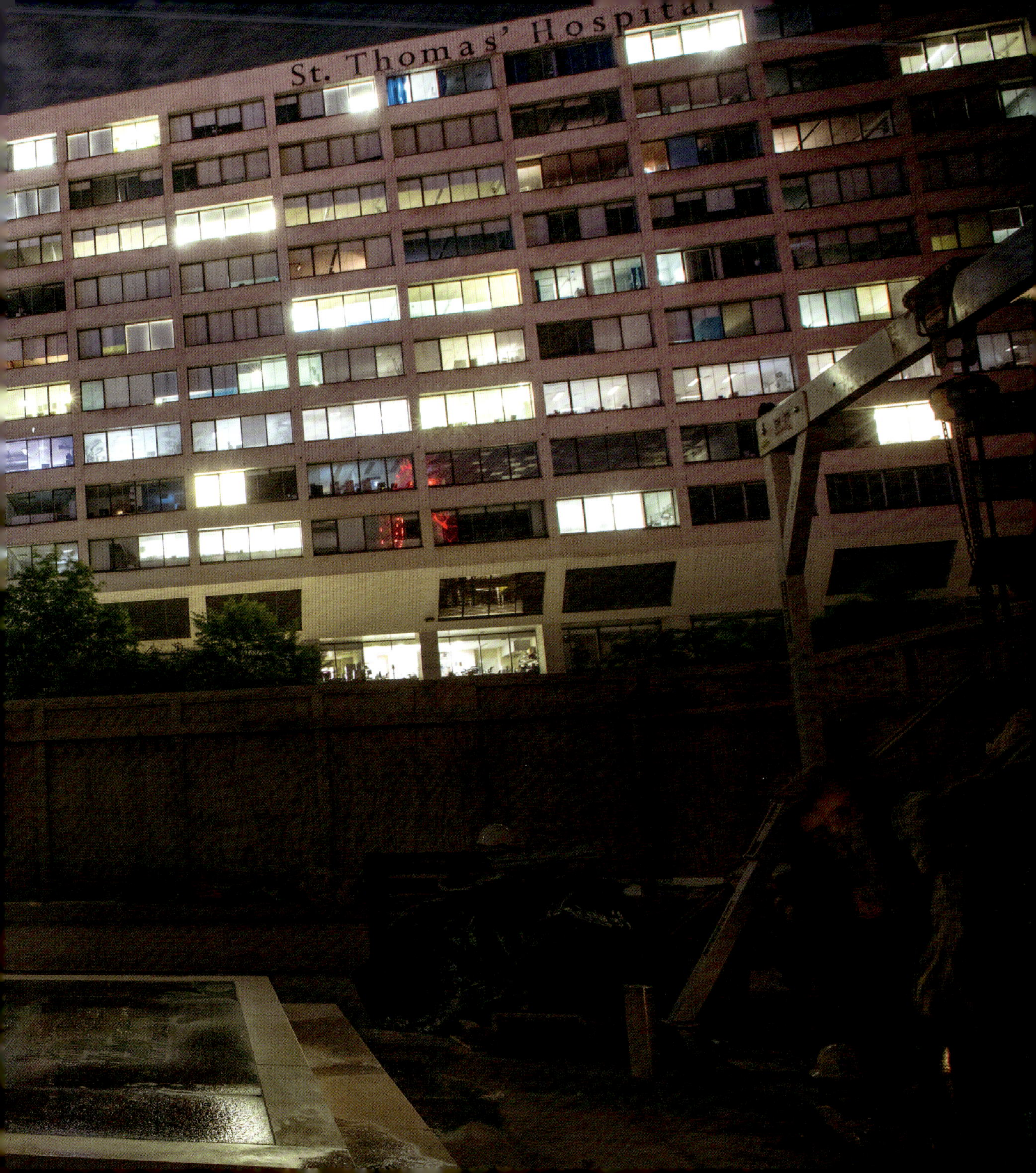
St. Thomas' Hospital

MARY SEACOLE
OFFICIAL STATUE UNVEILING
30 JUNE 2016 | 10.30AM - 1.00PM
ST THOMAS' HOSPITAL,
WESTMINSTER BRIDGE ROAD, LONDON

Programme design and photos by Jon Daniel

THE UNVEILING

Unveiled by Baroness Floella Benjamin, Deputy Lieutenant for Greater London

MARY
SEACOLE
MEMORIAL
STATUE APPEAL

105

MARY
SEACOLE
MEMORIAL
STATUE APPEAL

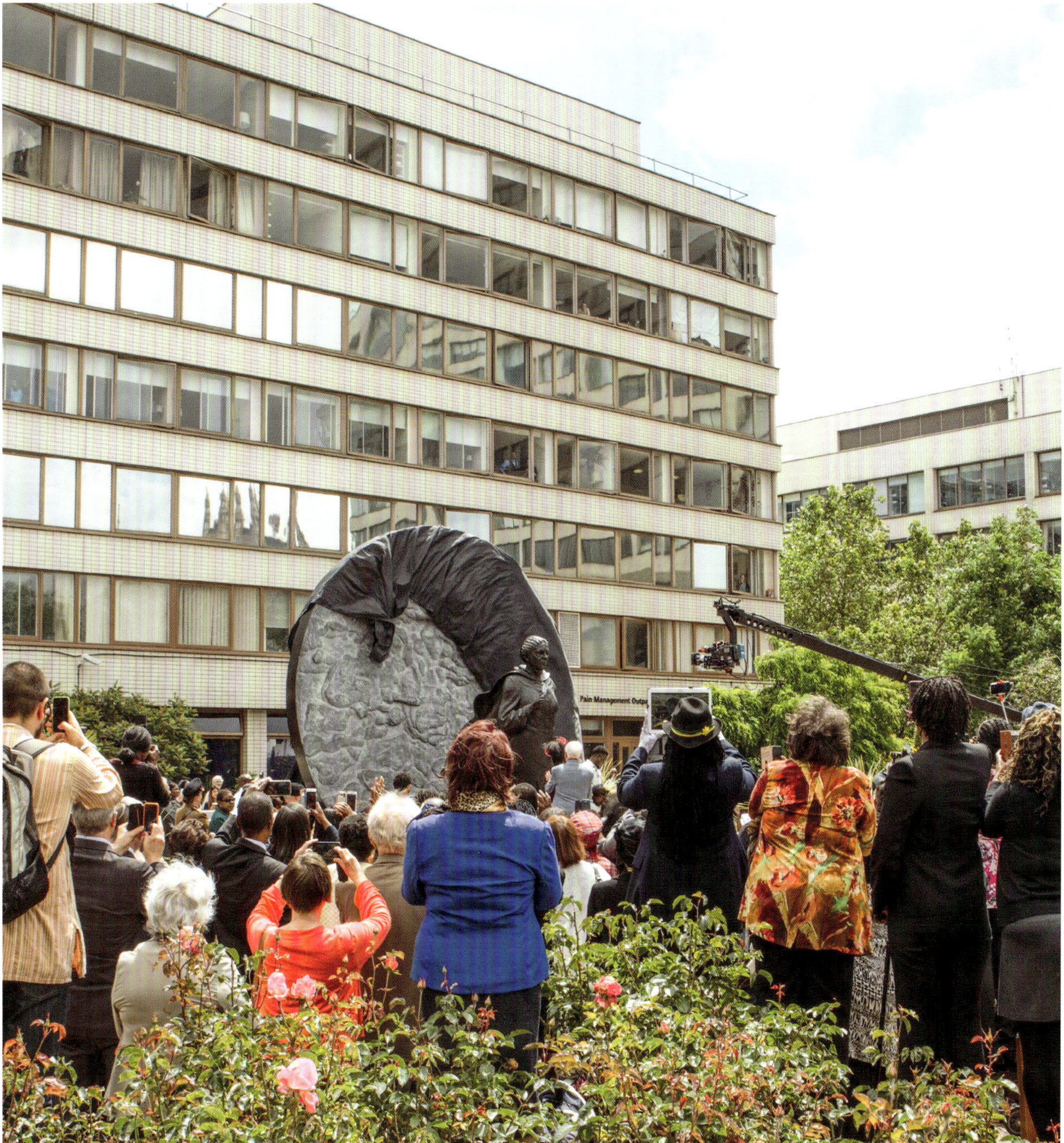

MARY
SEACOLE
MEMORIAL
STATUE APPEAL

109

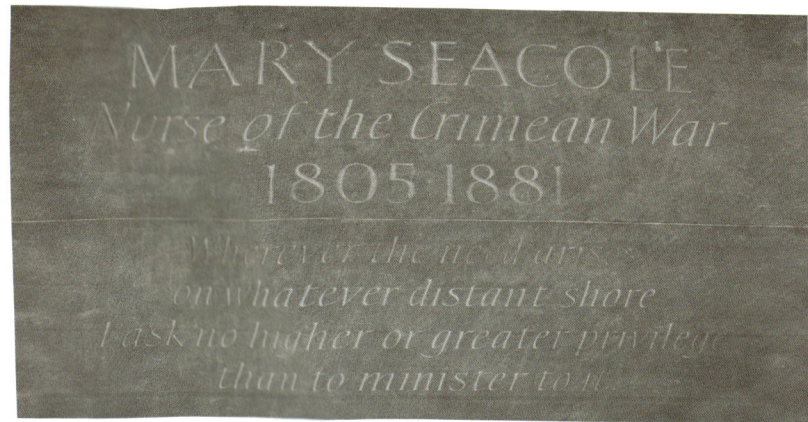

MARY
SEACOLE
MEMORIAL
STATUE APPEAL

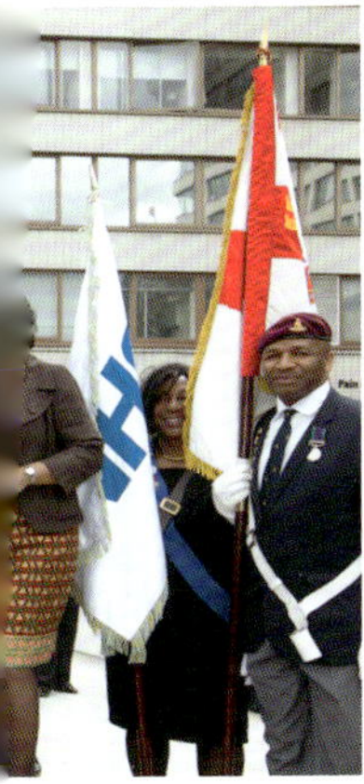

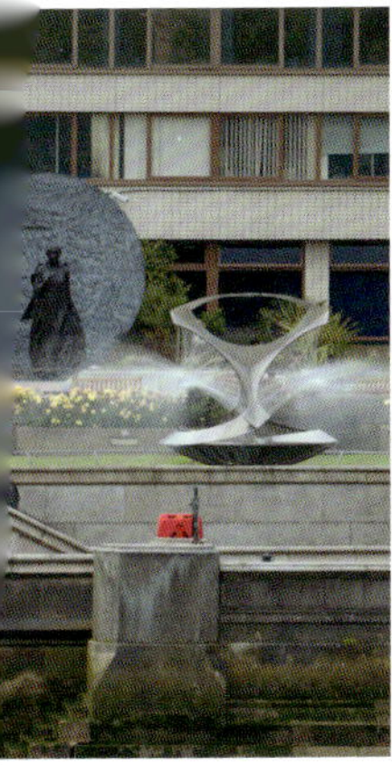

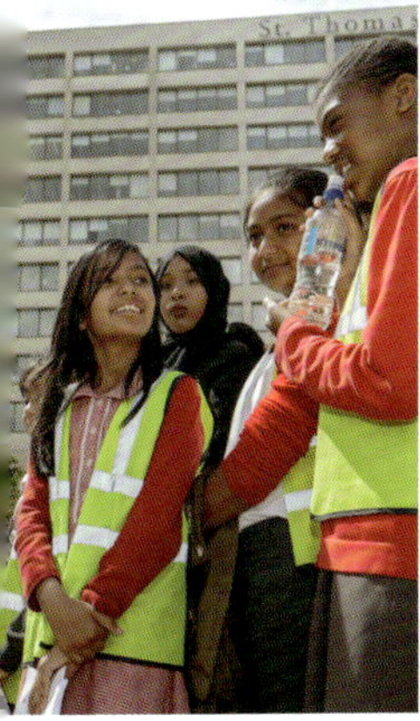
St. Thomas

MARY
SEACOLE
MEMORIAL
STATUE APPEAL

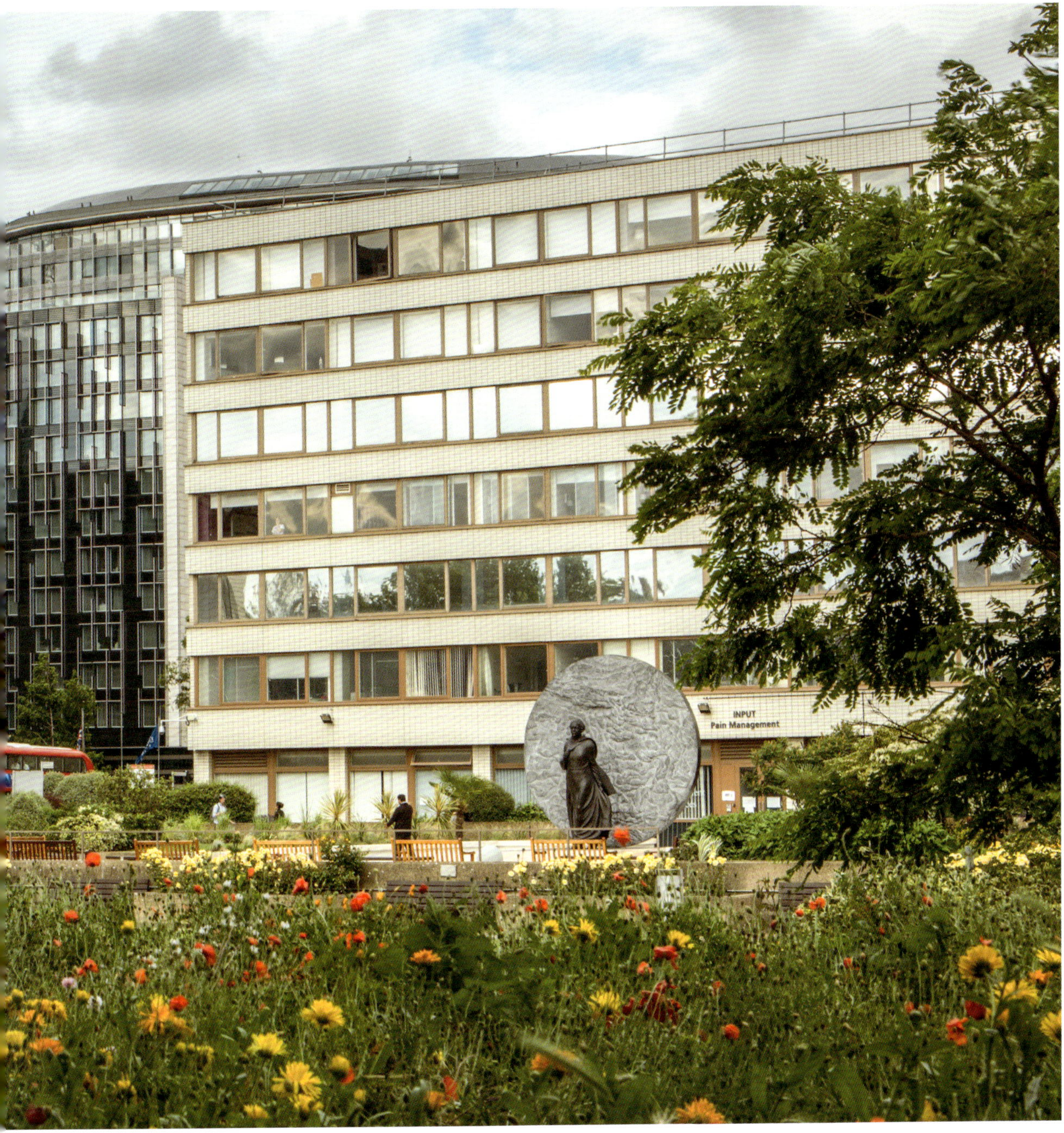
INPUT
Pain Management

THIS BRONZE DISC BEARS AN IMPRESSION
OF THE GROUND TAKEN FROM THE SITE IN CRIMEA
WHERE JAMAICAN NURSE MARY SEACOLE MINISTERED
TO BRITISH SOLDIERS DURING THE WAR OF 1853-1856

I trust that England will not forget one who nursed her sick who sought out her wounded to aid and succour them and who performed the last offices for some of her illustrious dead.

SIR WILLIAM HOWARD RUSSELL, WAR CORRESPONDENT, THE TIMES 1857

MARY SEACOLE MEMORIAL STATUE APPEAL

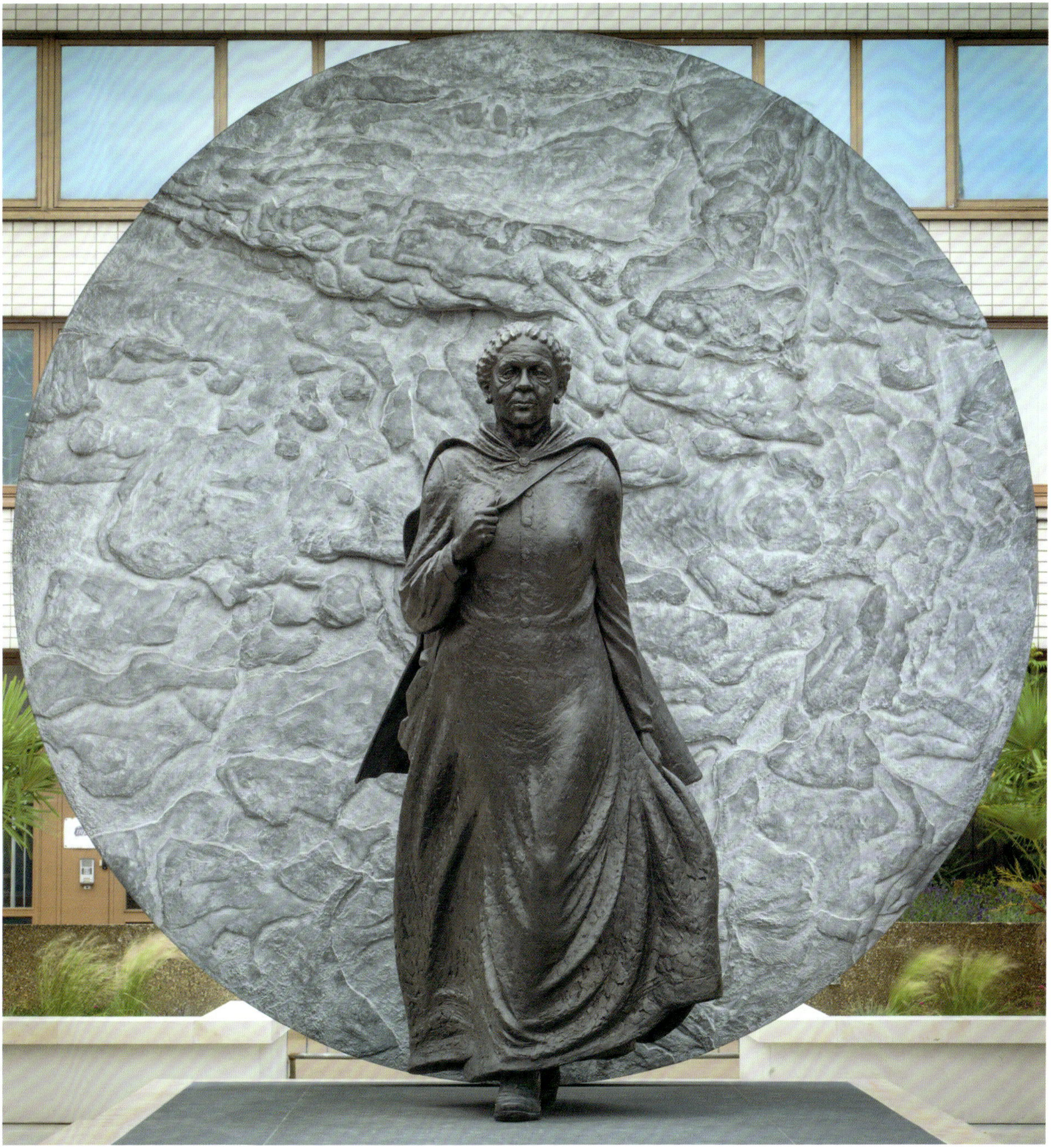

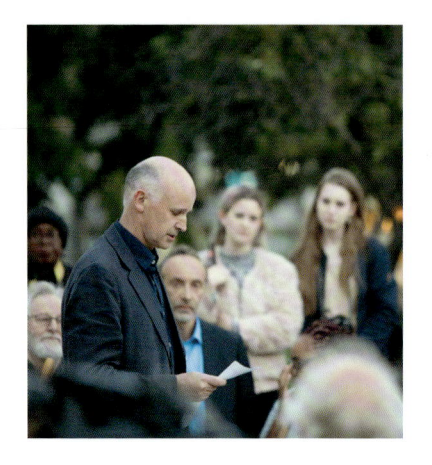

MARY
SEACOLE
MEMORIAL
STATUE APPEAL

117

MARY
SEACOLE
MEMORIAL
STATUE APPEAL

HM Treasury, 1 Horse Guards Road, London, SW1A 2HQ

11 June 2016

Lord Soley of Hammersmith
Chairman
Mary Seacole Memorial Statue Appeal
C/O Royal College of Nursing
20 Cavendish Square
London
W1G 0RN

Dear Clive,

Since 2012, I have made a series of banking fines announcements. Throughout all of these my intention has always been that the funds would be allocated to good causes including Military and Emergency Services charities and those that support personnel who represent the 'very best of values'.

I was therefore delighted to be able to assist the Mary Seacole Memorial Statue Appeal in their aims of erecting a memorial to Mary, the first memorial to a named black woman in this country, who throughout her life, epitomised those values; as well as to establish memorial gardens to Health Service personnel who have been killed or wounded in both conflict and danger zones.

Across the globe, men and women of the British military and civilian health services make an invaluable contribution to the health and welfare of others, often putting themselves in harm's way in the process. As a nation, we owe them an immense debt of gratitude and it is therefore particularly fitting that fines from those who have demonstrated the worst of values can be used to support this excellent cause.

Best wishes,

GEORGE OSBORNE

MARY
SEACOLE
MEMORIAL
STATUE APPEAL

ACKNOWLEDGEMENTS

This statue could not have been built without the support of thousands of individuals who have made donations or have taken part in fundraising events.

We have tried to ensure that we have thanked everyone who has played a major part in the evolution and creation of the Mary Seacole statue but it has been 13 years in planning and delivery so it is quite possible that some have slipped through the net. If so, we apologise profusely. We are a voluntary organisation without an office or employees. In any event we hope that everyone who has contributed will feel they have played a significant role in remembering Mary and creating a major work of art that came into being as a result of community action.

Thanks to the following organisations and individuals

Adamine

Matt Akid, Guy's and St Thomas' NHS Foundation Trust

Ann Alexander

Alexander Amosu

ANS

The Argyll and Sutherland Highlanders

Barbados Nurses Association Bridgetown

Barclays

Barclays Bank, Hounslow branch

Andrew Barnett

Beechcroft

The Big Push Ltd

Black Cultural Archives

British Heart Foundation

Rosslyn Brown

Estate of the late David Frank Burgess

Caribbean Broadcasting Corporation

Helen Carlyon

Channel 3 Group

Chelsea Football Club

Concerto

Coutts

Philomena Davidson. The Davidson Arts Partnership

Lucy Davis DAP Creative

Derek Hill Foundation

Dr Stephen Deuchar

Drax UK

Maurice W Facey, Pan-Jamaican Investment Trust

Florence Nightingale Museum

Florence Nightingale Foundation

Barbara Follett

Friendship House, 1 The Mall, Ealing Broadway, London W5 2 PJ

Sara Griffiths, PLMR

Guy's and St Thomas' NHS Foundation Trust

Lady Hollick

The Hollick Family Charitable Trust

Inter Service Group

Martin Jennings Ltd

Paul Johnson

Patrick Kennedy

9/12 Lancers (Prince of Wales's) Association

The Light Dragoons

Julia Langdon

Lodge Southern

Logix

London Adventist Chorale - fundraising concert

Nora Macleod

Ian MacTaggart Trust

Mary Seacole Memorial Association

Steve McGuire, Managing Director, Essentia, Guy's and St Thomas' NHS Foundation Trust

The Methodist Church Tithe

Miller Hare

Moore Blatch Solicitors

Joan Myers OBE

Norlands

Northmore

Nursing Association of Jamaica

Nursing Standard

O2 Brixton Academy

Adriana Paice

Pangolin Editions

Photofile Limited

Frances Pickersgill

Courtney Pine, Brixton event with: Jerry Deeney, The Portraits, Paper Faces, Capital Jors, Zita Holborne, Martin Furlong and Gail Adams

PLMR

Quality Medical Group

The Richard Rogers Charitable Settlement

Miss Yinka Rickford-Anguin

Road to Health Group

Robbi Robson

Rothschild Foundation

Royal College of Nursing

Paelo Saddler

Sandals Resorts International (Jamaica)

Christine Saunders, Steve Russell Studios

Selkirk Charitable Trust

Eleanor Smith, Unison

Lord Smith of Finsbury

Speirs + Major

Dr Reza Tabrizi

Carole Taylor

Sir Hugh Taylor, Chairman, Guy's and St Thomas' NHS Foundation Trust

Paulette and John Tomlinson

Unite

Unison

Unison Health Group

Unison Mid-Yorkshire Health Branch

The University of West London

Vantil Charles

Virgin Atlantic

Andrew Ward, Brunel University

Winstan Whitter, filmmaker

Military

Thanks to:

Second Lieutenant Keisha Bambury ACF, Officer Commanding 75 Detachment, Greater London South East Sector Army Cadet Force

Sergeant Johnson Beharry VC PWRR, courtesy of the Colonel of the Regiment, Brigadier Richard Dennis OBE

Major General Benjamin Bathurst, Major General Commanding the Household Division and General Officer Commanding London District

General Richard Dannatt, Baron Dannatt, GCB, CBE, MC, DL formerly Chief of the General Staff (2006 to 2008)

Sarah Goldthorpe, Editor, Soldier Magazine

Pipe Major Jim McLucas London Scottish, courtesy of the Commanding Officer The London Regiment Lieutenant Colonel Timothy Smart

Colonel Hugh Purcell, Chief Executive, Greater London Reserve Forces and Cadet Association

Colonel Marie Richter QARANC Commanding Officer 256 (London) Field Hospital,. Army Reserve Centre

Lieutenant Colonel James Senior LD, Commanding Officer, The Light Dragoons

Major General JHT Short CB OBE, 9/12 Lancers (Prince of Wales's) Association, Colonel of the Regiment

Debbie Wilkinson, Community Engagement Lead, Greater London Reserve Forces and Cadet Association

Major Colin Wood SCOTS, Officer Commanding Balaklava Company, Fifth Battalion, The Royal Regiment of Scotland, formerly The Argyll and Sutherland Highlanders (Princess Louise's)

Construction

Thanks to:

Sir Robert McAlpine Ltd
David McAlpine
James Campbell
David Norman
Mike O'Regan
Jamie Whiteaker
David Murray
Mike Murray

Bob Came
Tony Jolly
Henry Whitten
David Murray

McAlpine Design Group
Xin Jun Wang (designer)
Randal Ffrench
Suqlain Mahmood, Principal Designer under Construction Design Management

Realtime
Mike Keane
Eunan Campbell
Damien Gallagher

Szerelmey
John MacEachin
Mark Chivers
Lewis Matanle
Mark Merrick

Elstead Engineering
Andrew Wright
Paul Holland

Essentia
Geoff Talboys
Kevin O'Keeffe

Lighting
Speirs + Major

A Statue for Mary: the Seacole Legacy

Copyright © 2016 Mary Seacole Memorial Statue Appeal
www.maryseacoleappeal.org.uk

ISBN: 978-1-5262-0530-8
First published in Great Britain in 2016 by the Mary Seacole Memorial Statue Appeal

All rights reserved. No part of this publication may be reproduced or distributed in any form or by any means, or stored in a data base or retrieval system, without the prior written permission of the author.

Cover (illustration) by James Newton, courtesy of Speirs + Major
Photography by Steve Russell Studios Ltd, Martin Jennings and others
Designed by Steve Russell Studios Ltd
Printed in the United Kingdom by Healeys Printers